THE
NATURE OF
HISTORICAL
INQUIRY

THE NATURE OF HISTORICAL INQUIRY

Edited by **LEONARD M. MARSAK**

University of California, Santa Barbara

HOLT, RINEHART AND WINSTON

New York Chicago San Francisco Atlanta
Dallas Montreal Toronto London Sydney

Cover illustration: The Thinker, by Rodin.

(Photo by John King)

PREFACE

The college student has learned before he is well embarked on the serious study of history that history is more than the appropriate materials in the textbook. His instructor has no doubt provided him with supplementary source reading and will often argue from the source to his own conclusions independently of the text. On certain critical periods of history, like the French Revolution, the student might consult the various problem series and learn that there is a variety of interpretation of virtually every historical experience. He may even learn from such reading that there is as much revealed about the interpreter — his assumptions and biases, or those of his time and society — as there is about the events interpreted. But in none of these ways does the student learn that behind such argument lies more than a bewildering indecision on the part of historians, that the nature of historical inquiry demands such argument and inconclusiveness. Gradually he may sense that the uncertainty of history is one of the things he likes about it. Why history is uncertain, however, and what he derives from it perhaps he could not express. Others before him have been equally per-plexed by those questions.

It is useful, therefore, to introduce the undergraduate student to the philosophy of history in the hope that he will be guided to it more quickly than is normally the case. No attempt has been made in this book to cover all the theories of history or even to be entirely representative of the subjects considered here. My task is not that of *Philosophical Analysis and History* which Professor William H. Dray presents, or that of Hans Meyerhoff whose book *The Philosophy of History in Our Time* is at once more intensive and less extended than my own. Instead I am offering certain selected materials in the philosophy of history as I would define the subject under its major headings: metaphysics, methodology, and morality. I have also included a category called the meaning of history, because many historians and others have sought for one, although the quest has been largely abandoned in our own day, and, as we shall see, for good reason.

By now it should be clear that this book represents my own convictions about the philosophy of history. These are expressed in the part introductions that may be read as a general introduction to the book when taken all together, and as a summary of my views on the humanism of history. I would expect, however, that my position can and will be met by all varieties of objection when the student comes to test his own beliefs against it. It is not agreement that is asked of the student, but a suitable interplay of ideas about the questions raised here: Can we accurately remember the past? Are we ever able to forget it? Is history an autonomous branch of learning with epistemological problems of its own? Where or how should we look for meaning in history? What use or value does it have for us? The student's answers to these questions should provide him with a foundation for the self-conscious study of history, which is all we can ask of education itself.

My thanks go to Professor Burleigh T. Wilkins, whose suggestions have been valuable to me, and to my wife, Ann, who helped to clarify the introductions.

Santa Barbara, California   L. M. M.
October 1969

CONTENTS

1

MAN'S NATURE AND THE
STUDY OF HISTORY

In the selections that follow the problem of man and his
history is developed in a series of steps. If it is truly history,
Benedetto Croce argues, and not chronology or historical
antiquarianism that we are considering, then history must
have some relevance for the present. The past must be made
to speak to us now or it is not worth our attention. Of course,
Croce assumes that the past can and should be consulted for
an understanding of ourselves. On his view that we must
"conceive the relation of history to life as that of unity," it
follows that when we address ourselves to the past, we seek
solutions to problems that "come forth from the bosom of
life." Accordingly it is a short step from Croce, who tells us
that what is vital in our past is evident in the present, to Jose
Ortega y Gasset, who tells us that the present is in reality
little else but the past, that we carry the burden of history
with us always, if not consciously then unconsciously. Each
of us, for example, has been formed not only by our
families, but also in relation to the United States in which we
have grown up. America, however, can only be understood out
of its past, and that in relation to the history of Europe.
Through European history we make contact with the rest of
the world, directly as Europe made contact, and indirectly

through the similarities of human experience; so that to each one of us nothing human can ever be alien. Ortega confirms this view of history as one of the humanities by which we come to know ourselves. In studying history we are in a real sense defining ourselves as we might do in psychoanalysis, and with the same belief that out of our developing knowledge of who and what we are comes the power in some measure to control our lives. In what ways we may legitimately add to our lives through history remains to be seen.

If we accept that "man, in a word, has no nature, what he has is history," as Ortega puts it, and that history is forever in process, then how we come to describe the past is itself subject to change. Such being the case, it is important to know how we think about history, and especially how we think historically. Indeed, R. G. Collingwood suggests that we define history as being essentially a way of thinking. All history is the history of thought, he tells us, but more significantly, all thought is historical in character. "It is only by historical thinking that I can discover what I thought ten years ago, . . . or five minutes ago, by reflecting on an action that I then did, which surprised me when I realized what I had done. In this sense all knowledge of mind is historical." As for the historian, "his criterion of historical truth . . . is the idea of history itself: the idea of an imaginary picture of the past. That idea is . . . in Kantian language, **a priori**." Hence Collingwood concludes that history is an autonomous branch of learning with epistemological problems of its own. The historian "can never say that his picture of the past is at any point adequate to his idea of what it ought to be. But, however fragmentary and faulty the results of his work may be, the idea which governed its course is clear, rational, and universal. It is the idea of the historical imagination as a self-dependent, self-determining, and self-justifying form of thought." It seems that like Molière's **Bourgeois Gentil-homme** who discovered that he was speaking prose, we have been thinking historically all our lives without knowing it.

BENEDETTO CROCE

History and Chronicle

"Contemporary history" is wont to be called the history of a passage of time, looked upon as a most recent past, whether it be that of the last fifty years, a decade, a year, a month, a day, or indeed of the last hour or of the last minute. But if we think and speak rigorously, the term "contemporaneous" can be applied only to that history which comes into being immediately after the act which is being accomplished, as consciousness of that act: it is, for instance, the history that I make of myself while I am in the act of composing these pages; it is the thought of my composition, linked of necessity to the work of composition. "Contemporary" would be well employed in this case, just because this, like every act of the spirit, is outside time (of the first and after) and is formed "at the same time" as the act to which it is linked, and from which it is distinguished by means of a distinction not chronological but ideal. "Non-contemporary history," "past history," would, on the other hand, be that which finds itself in the presence of a history already formed, and which thus comes into being as a criticism of that history, whether it be thousands of years or hardly an hour old.

From Benedetto Croce, *History: Its Theory and Practice,* translated by Douglas Ainslie (New York: Harcourt, Brace & Company, 1921), pp. 11–15.

3

But if we look more closely, we perceive that this history already formed, which is called or which we would like to call "non-contemporary" or "past" history, if it really is history, that is to say, if it means something and is not an empty echo, is also *contemporary,* and does not in any way differ from the other. As in the former case, the condition of its existence is that the deed of which the history is told must vibrate in the soul of the historian, or (to employ the expression of professed historians) that the documents are before the historian and that they are intelligible. That a narrative or a series of narratives of the fact is united and mingled with it merely means that the fact has proved more rich, not that it has lost its quality of being present: what were narratives or judgments before are now themselves facts, "documents" to be interpreted and judged. History is never constructed from narratives, but always from documents, or from narratives that have been reduced to documents and treated as such. Thus if contemporary history springs straight from life, so too does that history which is called non-contemporary, for it is evident that only an interest in the life of the present can move one to investigate past fact. Therefore this past fact does not answer to a past interest, but to a present interest, in so far as it is unified with an interest of the present life. This has been said again and again in a hundred ways by historians in their empirical formulas, and constitutes the reason, if not the deeper content, of the success of the very trite saying that history is *magister vitae.*

I have recalled these forms of historical technique in order to remove the aspect of paradox from the proposition that "every true history is contemporary history." But the justice of this proposition is easily confirmed and copiously and perspicuously exemplified in the reality of historiographical work, provided always that we do not fall into the error of taking the works of the historians all together, or certain groups of them confusedly, and of applying them to an abstract man or to ourselves considered abstractly, and of then asking what present interest leads to the writing or reading of such histories: for instance, what is the present interest of the history which recounts the Peloponnesian or the Mithradatic War, of the events connected with Mexican art, or with Arabic philosophy. For me at the present moment they are without interest, and therefore for me at this present moment those histories are not histories, but at the most simply titles of historical works. They have been or will be histories in those that have thought or will think them, and in me too when I have thought or shall think them, re-elaborating them according to my spiritual needs. If, on the other hand, we limit ourselves to real history, to the history that one really thinks in the act of thinking, it will be easily seen that this is perfectly identical with the most personal and contemporary of histories. When the development of the culture of my historical moment presents to me (it would be superfluous and perhaps also inexact to add to myself as an individual) the problem of Greek civilization or of Platonic philosophy or of a particular mode of Attic manners, that problem is related to my being in the same way as the history of a bit of business in which I am engaged, or of a love affair in which I am indulging, or of a danger that threatens me. I examine it with the same anxiety and am troubled with the same sense of unhappiness until I have succeeded in solving it. Hellenic life is on that occasion present in me; it solicits, it attracts and torments me, in the same way as the appearance of the adversary, of the loved one, or of the beloved son for whom one trembles. Thus too it happens or has happened or will happen in the case of the Mithradatic War, of Mexican art, and of all the other things that I have mentioned above by way of example.

Having laid it down that contemporaneity is not the characteristic of a class of histories (as is held with good reason in empirical classifications), but an intrinsic characteristic of every history, we must conceive the relation of history to life as that of *unity*; certainly not in the sense of abstract identity, but of synthetic unity, which implies both the distinction and the unity of the terms. Thus to talk of a history of which the documents are lacking would appear to be as extravagant as to talk of the existence of something as to which it is also affirmed that it is without one of the essential conditions of existence. A history without relation to the document would be an unverifiable history; and since the reality of history lies in this verifiability, and the narrative in which it is given concrete form is historical narrative only in so far as it is a *critical exposition* of the document (intuition and reflection, consciousness and auto-consciousness, etc.), a history of that sort, being without meaning and without truth, would be inexistent as history. How could a history of painting be composed by one who had not seen and enjoyed the works of which he proposed to describe the genesis critically? And how far could anyone understand the works in question who was without the artistic experience assumed by the narrator? How could there be a history of philosophy without the works or at least fragments of the works of the philosophers? How could there be a history of a sentiment or of a custom, for example that of Christian humility or of knightly chivalry, without the capacity for living again, or rather without an actual living again of these particular states of the individual soul?

On the other hand, once the indissoluble link between life and thought in history has been effected, the doubts that have been expressed as to the *certainty* and the *utility* of history disappear altogether in a moment. How could that which is a *present* producing of our spirit ever be *uncertain?* How could that knowledge be *useless* which solves a problem that has come forth from the bosom of *life?* . . .

JOSE ORTEGA Y GASSET

History as a System

Man, in a word, has no nature; what he has is . . . history.
Expressed differently: what nature is to things, history, *res gestae,*
is to man. Once again we become aware of the possible application of theological concepts to human reality. *Deus, cui hoc est
natura quod fecerit* . . . , says St. Augustine.[1] Man, likewise, finds
that he has no nature other than what he has himself done.

It is comic in the extreme that "historicism" should be condemned because it produces or corroborates in us the consciousness that the human factor is changeable in its every direction,
that in it there is nothing concrete that is stable. As if the stable
being—the stone, for instance—were preferable to the unstable!
"Substantial" mutation is the condition on which an entity as such
can be progressive, the condition on which its being may consist
in progress. Now concerning man it must be said, not only that his
being is variable, but also that his being grows and, in this sense,
that it progresses. The error of the old doctrine of progress lay in

---

[1] *De Genesi ad litteram, vi,* 13.24 *(Patrologia Latine,* vol. 34).

affirming *a priori* that man progresses towards the better. That is something that can only be determined *a posteriori* by concrete historical reason: it is precisely the great discovery we await from this, since to it we look for the clarifying of human reality and, along with this, for light on the nature of the good, the bad, the better, and the worse. But that our life does possess a simply progressive character, this we can affirm *a priori* with full evidence and with a surety very different from that which has led to the supposition of the improgressivity of nature, that is to say, the "invariability of its laws." The same knowledge that discovers to us man's variation makes patent his progressive consistency. The European of today is not only different from what he was fifty years ago; his being now includes that of fifty years ago. The European of today finds himself without a living faith in science precisely *because* fifty years ago he did believe wholeheartedly in it. That faith that held sway half a century ago may now be defined with reasonable precision; were this done it would be seen that it was such *because* about 1800 the same faith in science wore a different profile, and so successively until we come to the year 1700 or thereabouts, at which date faith in reason is constituted as a "collective belief," as something socially operative. (Earlier than 1700 faith in reason is an individual belief or the belief of particular small groups that live submerged in societies where faith in God, if already more or less inert, yet continues operative.) In our present "crisis," in our present doubt concerning reason, we find then included the whole of that earlier life. We are, that is to say, all those forms of faith in reason, and we are in addition the doubt engendered by that faith. We are other than the man of 1700, and we are more.

There is no cause, therefore, for weeping overmuch concerning the mutability of everything human. This is precisely our ontological privilege. Progress is only possible to one who is not linked today to what he was yesterday, who is not caught for ever in that being which is already, but can migrate from it into another. But this is not enough: it is not sufficient that man should be able to free himself from what he is already and take on a new form, as the serpent sloughs its skin and is left with another. Progress demands that this new form should rise above the old and to this end should preserve it and turn it to account, that it should take off from the old, climbing on its shoulders as a high temperature mounts on lower ones. To progress is to accumulate being, to store up reality. This increase of being, it is true, when referred only to the individual, might be interpreted naturalistically as the mere development or *enodatio* of an initial disposition. With the evolutionary thesis still unproved, whatever its probability, it can be said that the tiger of today is neither more nor less a tiger than was that of a thousand years ago: it is being a tiger for the first time, it is always a first tiger. But the human individual is not putting on humanity for the first time. To begin with, he finds around him, in his "circumstance," other men and the society they give rise to. Hence his humanity, that which begins to develop in him, takes its point of departure from another, already developed, that has reached its culmination: in short, to his humanity he adds other humanities. He finds at birth a form of humanity, a mode of being a man, already forged, that he need not invent but may simply take over and set out from for his individual development. This does not begin for him—as for the tiger, which must always start again—at zero but at a positive quantity to which he adds his own growth. Man is not a first man, an eternal Adam: he is formally a second man, a third man, etc.

Mutable condition has thus its ontological virtue and grace, and invites one to recall Galileo's words: *I detrattori della corruttibilità meriterebber d'esser cangiati in statue.*

Let the reader reflect closely on his life, studying it against the light as one looks at a glass of water to study its infusoria. If he asks himself why his life is thus and not otherwise, it will appear to him that not a few details had their origin in inscrutable chance. But he will find the broad lines of its reality perfectly comprehensible once he sees that he is thus because, in the last resort, the society—"collective man"—in which he lives is thus. And in its turn the mode of being of society will stand revealed, once there is discovered within it what that society was—what it believed, felt, preferred—at an earlier stage. That is to say that in his individual and fleeting today man will see, foreshortened, the whole of man's past still active and alive. For we can only throw light on yesterday by invoking the day before yesterday; and so with all yesterdays. History is a system, the system of human experiences linked in a single, inexorable chain. Hence nothing can be truly clear in history until everything is clear. We cannot properly understand what this "rationalist" European is unless we know exactly what it was to be a Christian, nor what it was to be a Christian unless we know what it was to be a Stoic: and so the process goes on. And this systematism of *res gestae* becomes reoperative and potent in history as *cognitio rerum gestarum.* Every historic term whatsoever, to have exactness, must be determined as a function of all history, neither more nor less than each concept in Hegel's *Logic* has value only in respect of the niche left for it by the others.

History is the systematic science of that radical reality, my life. It is therefore a science of the present in the most rigorous and actual sense of the word. Were it not a science of the present, where should we find that past that is commonly assigned to it as theme? The opposite—and customary—interpretation is equivalent to making of the past an abstract, unreal something lying lifeless just where it happened in time, whereas the past is in truth the live, active force that sustains our today. There is no *actio in distans.* The past is not yonder, at the date when it happened, but here, in me. The past is I— by which I mean my life.

R. G. COLLINGWOOD

The Idea of History

My answer is that history is "for" human self-knowledge. It is generally thought to be of importance to man that he should know himself: where knowing himself means knowing not his merely personal peculiarities, the things that distinguish him from other men, but his nature as man. Knowing yourself means knowing, first, what it is to be a man; secondly, knowing what it is to be the kind of man you are; and thirdly, knowing what it is to be the man *you* are and nobody else is. Knowing yourself means knowing what you can do; and since nobody knows what he can do until he tries, the only clue to what man can do is what man has done. The value of history, then, is that it teaches us what man has done and thus what man is . . . .

The processes of nature can be properly described as sequences of mere events, but those of history cannot. They are not processes of mere events but processes of actions, which have an inner side, consisting of processes of thought; and what the historian is looking for is these processes of thought. All history is the history of thought . . . . The historian not only re-enacts past

From R. G. Collingwood, *The Idea of History* (New York: Oxford University Press, 1956), pp. 10, 215–216, 218–219, 247–249, 251–252, 257–258, 269–270, 275, 292, 305, 328–329, 333–334. Reprinted by permission of The Clarendon Press, Oxford.

11

thought, he re-enacts it in the context of his own knowledge and therefore, in re-enacting it, criticizes it, forms his own judgment of its value, corrects whatever errors he can discern in it. This criticism of the thought whose history he traces is not something secondary to tracing the history of it. It is an indispensable condition of the historical knowledge itself. Nothing could be a completer error concerning the history of thought than to suppose that the historian as such merely ascertains "what so-and-so thought," leaving it to someone else to decide "whether it was true." All thinking is critical thinking; the thought which re-enacts past thoughts, therefore, criticizes them in re-enacting them . . . .

Historical knowledge is the knowledge of what mind has done in the past, and at the same time it is the redoing of this, the perpetuation of past acts in the present. Its object is therefore not a mere object, something outside the mind which knows it; it is an activity of thought, which can be known only in so far as the knowing mind re-enacts it and knows itself as so doing. To the historian, the activities whose history he is studying are not spectacles to be watched, but experiences to be lived through in his own mind; they are objective, or known to him, only because they are also subjective, or activities of his own.

It may thus be said that historical inquiry reveals to the historian the powers of his own mind. Since all he can know historically is thoughts that he can re-think for himself, the fact of his coming to know them shows him that his mind is able (or by the very effort of studying them has become able) to think in these ways. And conversely, whenever he finds certain historical matters unintelligible, he has discovered a limitation of his own mind; he has discovered that there are certain ways in which he is not, or no longer, or not yet, able to think. Certain historians, sometimes whole generations of historians, find in certain periods of history nothing intelligible, and call them dark ages; but such phrases tell us nothing about those ages themselves, though they tell us a great deal about the persons who use them, namely that they are unable to re-think the thoughts which were fundamental to their life . . . .

But historical knowledge is not concerned only with a remote past. If it is by historical thinking that we re-think and so redis-

cover the thought of Hammurabi or Solon, it is in the same way
that we discover the thought of a friend who writes us a letter, or
a stranger who crosses the street. Nor is it necessary that the
historian should be one person and the subject of his inquiry
another. It is only by historical thinking that I can discover what I
thought ten years ago, by reading what I then wrote, or what I
thought five minutes ago, by reflecting on an action that I then
did, which surprised me when I realized what I had done. In this
sense, all knowledge of mind is historical . . . .

The whole perceptible world, then, is potentially and in principle evidence to the historian. It becomes actual evidence in so far
as he can use it. And he cannot use it unless he comes to it with
the right kind of historical knowledge. The more historical knowledge we have, the more we can learn from any given piece of
evidence; if we had none, we could learn nothing. Evidence is
evidence only when some one contemplates it historically. Otherwise it is merely perceived fact, historically dumb. It follows that
historical knowledge can only grow out of historical knowledge; in
other words, that historical thinking is an original and fundamental activity of the human mind, or, as Descartes might have said,
that the idea of the past is an "innate" idea.

Historical thinking is that activity of the imagination by which
we endeavour to provide this innate idea with detailed content.
And this we do by using the present as evidence for its own past.
Every present has a past of its own, and any imaginative recon-
struction of the past aims at reconstructing the past of this
present, the present in which the act of imagination is going on, as
here and now perceived. In principle the aim of any such act is to
use the entire perceptible here-and-now as evidence for the entire
past through whose process it has come into being. In practice,
this aim can never be achieved. The perceptible here-and-now
can never be perceived, still less interpreted, in its entirety; and
the infinite process of past time can never be envisaged as a
whole. But this separation between what is attempted in principle
and what is achieved in practice is the lot of mankind, not a
peculiarity of historical thinking. The fact that it is found there
only shows that herein history is like art, science, philosophy, the
pursuit of virtue, and the search for happiness.

It is for the same reason that in history, as in all serious matters, no achievement is final. The evidence available for solving any given problem changes with every change of historical method and with every variation in the competence of historians. The principles by which this evidence is interpreted change too; since the interpreting of evidence is a task to which a man must bring everything he knows: historical knowledge, knowledge of nature and man, mathematical knowledge, philosophical knowledge; and not knowledge only, but mental habits and possessions of every kind: and none of these is unchanging. Because of these changes, which never cease, however slow they may appear to observers who take a short view, every new generation must rewrite history in its own way; every new historian, not content with giving new answers to old questions, must revise the questions themselves; and—since historical thought is a river into which none can step twice—even a single historian, working at a single subject for a certain length of time, finds when he tries to reopen an old question that the question has changed.

This is not an argument for historical scepticism. It is only the discovery of a second dimension of historical thought, the history of history: the discovery that the historian himself, together with the here-and-now which forms the total body of evidence available to him, is a part of the process he is studying, has his own place in that process, and can see it only from the point of view which at this present moment he occupies within it.

But neither the raw material of historical knowledge, the detail of the here-and-now as given him in perception, nor the various endowments that serve him as aids to interpreting this evidence, can give the historian his criterion of historical truth. That criterion is the idea of history itself: the idea of an imaginary picture of the past. That idea is, in Cartesian language, innate; in Kantian language, *a priori*. It is not a chance product of psychological causes; it is an idea which every man possesses as part of the furniture of his mind, and discovers himself to possess in so far as he becomes conscious of what it is to have a mind. Like other ideas of the same sort, it is one to which no fact of experience exactly corresponds. The historian, however long and faithfully he works, can never say that his work, even in crudest outline or in this or that smallest detail, is done once for all. He can never say that his picture of the past is at any point adequate to his idea of what it ought to be. But, however fragmentary and faulty the results of his work may be, the idea which governed its course is clear, rational, and universal. It is the idea of the historical imagination as a self-dependent, self-determining, and self-justifying form of thought. . . .

History is a science, but a science of a special kind. It is a science whose business is to study events not accessible to our observation, and to study these events inferentially, arguing to them from something else which is accessible to our observation, and which the historian calls "evidence" for the events in which he is interested . . . .

There is a kind of history which depends altogether upon the testimony of authorities. As I have already said, it is not really history at all, but we have no other name for it. The method by which it proceeds is first to decide what we want to know about, and then to go in search of statements about it, oral or written, purporting to be made by actors in the events concerned, or by eyewitnesses of them, or by persons repeating what actors or eyewitnesses have told them, or have told their informants, or those who informed their informants, and so on. Having found in such a statement something relevant to his purpose, the historian excerpts it and incorporates it, translated if necessary and recast into what he considers a suitable style, in his own history. As a rule, where he has many statements to draw upon, he will find that one of them tells him what another does not; so both or all of them will be incorporated. Sometimes he will find that one of them contradicts another; then, unless he can find a way of reconciling them, he must decide to leave one out; and this, if he is conscientious, will involve him in a critical consideration of the contradictory authorities' relative degree of trustworthiness. And sometimes one of them, or possibly even all of them, will tell him a story which he simply cannot believe, a story characteristic, perhaps, of the superstitions or prejudices of the author's time or the circle in which he lived, but not credible to a more enlightened age, and therefore to be omitted.

History constructed by excerpting and combining the testimonies of different authorities I call scissors-and-paste history. I repeat that it is not really history at all, because it does not satisfy the necessary conditions of science; but until lately it was the only kind of history in existence, and a great deal of the history people are still reading to-day, and even a good deal of what people are still writing, belongs to this type. Consequently people who know little about history (some of whom, in spite of my recent farewell, may still be reading these pages) will say with some impatience: "Why, this thing that you say is not history, is just history itself; scissors and paste, that is what history is; and that is why history is not a science, which is a fact that everybody knows, in spite of groundless claims by professional historians magnifying their office. . . ."

Francis Bacon, lawyer and philosopher, laid it down in one of his memorable phrases that the natural scientist must "put Nature to the question." What he was denying, when he wrote this, was that the scientist's attitude towards nature should be one of respectful attentiveness, waiting upon her utterances and building his theories on the basis of what she chose to vouchsafe him. What he was asserting was two things at once: first, that the scientist must take the initiative, deciding for himself what he wants to know and formulating this in his own mind in the shape of a question; and secondly, that he must find means of compelling nature to answer, devising tortures under which she can no longer hold her tongue. Here, in a single brief epigram, Bacon laid down once for all the true theory of experimental science.

It is also, though Bacon did not know this, the true theory of historical method. In scissors-and-paste history the historian takes up a pre-Baconian position. His attitude towards his authorities, as the very word shows, is one of respectful attentiveness. He waits to hear what they choose to tell him, and lets them tell it in their own way and at their own time. Even when he has invented historical criticism, and his authorities have become mere sources, this attitude is at bottom unchanged. There is a change, but it is only superficial. It consists merely in the adoption of a technique for dividing witnesses into sheep and goats. One class is disqualified from giving testimony; the other is treated exactly as authorities were treated under the old dispensation. But in scientific history, or history proper, the Baconian revolution has been accomplished. The scientific historian no doubt spends a great deal of time reading the same books that the scissors-and-paste historian used to read—Herodotus, Thucydides, Livy, Tacitus, and so forth—but he reads them in an entirely different spirit; in fact, a Baconian spirit. The scissors-and-paste historian reads them in a simply receptive spirit, to find out what they said. The scientific historian reads them with a question in his mind, having taken the initiative by deciding for himself what he wants to find out from them. Further, the scissors-and-paste historian reads them on the understanding that what they did not tell him in so many words he would never find out from them at all; the scientific historian puts them to the torture, twisting a passage ostensibly about something quite different into an answer to the question he has decided to ask. . . .

It follows that scientific history contains no ready-made statements at all. The act of incorporating a ready-made statement into the body of his own historical knowledge is an act which, for a scientific historian, is impossible. Confronted with a ready-made statement about the subject he is studying, the scientific historian never asks himself: "Is this statement true or false?" in other words "Shall I incorporate it in my history of that subject or not?" The question he asks himself is: "What does this statement mean?" And this is not equivalent to the question "What did the person who made it mean by it?" although that is doubtless a question that the historian must ask, and must be able to answer. It is equivalent, rather, to the question "What light is thrown on the subject in which I am interested by the fact that this person made this statement, meaning by it what he did mean?" This might be expressed by saying that the scientific historian does not treat statements as statements but as evidence: not as true or false accounts of the facts of which they profess to be accounts, but as other facts which, if he knows the right questions to ask about them, may throw light on those facts . . . .

The act of thinking, then, is not only subjective but objective as well. It is not only a thinking, it is something that can be thought about. But, because (as I have already tried to show) it is never merely objective, it requires to be thought about in a peculiar way, a way only appropriate to itself. It cannot be set before the thinking mind as a ready-made object, discovered as something independent of that mind and studied as it is in itself, in that independence. It can never be studied "objectively," in the sense in which "objectively" excludes "subjectively." It has to be studied as it actually exists, that is to say, as an act. And because this act is subjectivity (though not mere subjectivity) or experience, it can be studied only in its own subjective being, that is, by the thinker whose activity or experience it is. This study is not mere experience or consciousness, not even mere self-consciousness: it is self-knowledge. Thus the act of thought in becoming subjective does not cease to be objective; it is the object of a self-knowledge which differs from mere consciousness in being self-consciousness or awareness, and differs from being mere self-consciousness in being self-knowledge: the critical study of one's own thought, not the mere awareness of that thought as one's own. . . .

If the historian, working against the grain of his own mind because it is demanded of him that he should study such uncongenial subjects, or because they are "in the period" which his own misguided conscience fancies he ought to treat in all its aspects, tries to master the history of a thought into which he cannot personally enter, instead of writing its history he will merely repeat the statements that record the external facts of its development: names and dates, and ready-made descriptive phrases. Such repetitions may very well be useful, but not because they are history. They are dry bones, which may some day become history, when someone is able to clothe them with the flesh and blood of a thought which is both his own and theirs. This is only a way of saying that the historian's thought must spring from the organic unity of his total experience, and be a function of his entire personality with its practical as well as its theoretical interests. It need hardly be added that since the historian is a son of his time, there is a general likelihood that what interests him will interest his contemporaries. It is a familiar fact that every generation finds itself interested in, and therefore able to study historically, tracts and aspects of the past which to its fathers were dry bones, signifying nothing.

Historical knowledge, then, has for its proper object thought: not things thought about, but the act of thinking itself . . . .

The old dogma of a single historical progress leading to the present, and the modern dogma of historical cycles, that is, of a multiple progress leading to "great ages" and then to decadence, are thus mere projections of the historian's ignorance upon the screen of the past. But, setting dogmas aside, has the idea of progress no other basis than this? We have already seen that there is one condition on which that idea can represent a genuine thought, and not either a blind feeling or a mere state of ignorance. The condition is that the person who uses the word should use it in comparing two historical periods or ways of life, both of which he can understand historically, that is, with enough sympathy and insight to reconstruct their experience for himself. He must satisfy himself and his readers that no blind spot in his own mind, and no defect in his equipment of learning, prevents him from entering into the experience of either less fully than into the other's. Then, having fulfilled that condition, he is entitled to ask whether the change from the first to the second was a progress.

But when he asks this, what exactly is he asking? Obviously, he is not asking whether the second comes nearer to the way of life which he accepts as his own. By re-enacting the experience of either in his own mind he has already accepted it as a thing to be judged by its own standards: a form of life having its own problems, to be judged by its success in solving those problems and no others. Nor is he assuming that the two different ways of life were attempts to do one and the same thing, and asking whether the second did it better than the first. Bach was not trying to write like Beethoven and failing; Athens was not a relatively unsuccessful attempt to produce Rome; Plato was himself, not a half-developed Aristotle.

There is only one genuine meaning for this question. If thought in its first phase, after solving the initial problems of that phase, is then, through solving these, brought up against others which defeat it; and if the second solves these further problems without losing its hold on the solution of the first, so that there is gain without any corresponding loss, then there is progress. And there can be progress on no other terms. If there is any loss, the problem of setting loss against gain is insoluble . . . . For progress is not a mere fact to be discovered by historical thinking: it is only through historical thinking that it comes about at all.

The reason for this is that progress, in those cases (common or rare) when it happens, happens only in one way: by the retention in the mind, at one phase, of what was achieved in the preceding phase. The two phases are related not merely by way of succession, but by way of continuity, and continuity of a peculiar kind. If Einstein makes an advance on Newton, he does it by knowing Newton's thought and retaining it within his own, in the sense that he knows what Newton's problems were, and how he solved them, and, disentangling the truth in those solutions from whatever errors prevented Newton from going further, embodying these solutions as thus disentangled in his own theory. He might have done this, no doubt, without having read Newton in the original for himself; but not without having received Newton's doctrine from someone. Thus Newton stands, in such a context, not for a man but for a theory, reigning during a certain period of scientific thought. It is only in so far as Einstein knows that theory, as a fact in the history of science, that he can make an advance upon it. Newton thus lives in Einstein in the way in which any past experience lives in the mind of the historian, as a past experience known as past—as the point from which the development with which he is concerned started—but re-enacted here and now together with a development of itself that is partly constructive or positive and partly critical or negative.

Similarly with any other progress. If we want to abolish capitalism or war, and in doing so not only to destroy them but to bring into existence something better, we must begin by understanding them: seeing what the problems are which our economic or international system succeeds in solving, and how the solution of these is related to the other problems which it fails to solve. This understanding of the system we set out to supersede is a thing which we must retain throughout the work of superseding it, as a knowledge of the past conditioning our creation of the future. It may be impossible to do this; our hatred of the thing we are destroying may prevent us from understanding it, and we may love it so much that we cannot destroy it unless we are blinded by such hatred. But if that is so, there will once more, as so often in the past, be change but no progress; we shall have lost our hold on one group of problems in our anxiety to solve the next. And we ought by now to realize that no kindly law of nature will save us from the fruits of our ignorance.

2

METHODS OF HISTORICAL INQUIRY

R. G. Collingwood said of history that it is essentially an expression of ideas and not merely the chronicling of fact. He was forced then to address himself to the epistemological problems of history and in doing so found that history's rules of evidence are like those of science, although history's results are perhaps not so sure. Leaving aside the fact that man's techniques in the various disciplines have grown more "scientific" in time, what does it mean to distinguish between matter and method in history? Obviously in comparing science with history, much depends on what one means by both. Science achieves more dependable results than history, but Collingwood insists that history is like science in providing us with provisional truths that are provable, if at all, only in the future when all the evidence will be in. In addition, we might say that history like science rests on an assumption of uniformity, not of nature in this case but of man, whose motives we may deem alike in all times and places. Both disciplines aspire to generalized statements of explanation that are forever open to exception. Thus history and science are equally unable to say something that is at once true and complete. If scientific truth is not absolute, that is all the more reason to be satisfied with less than absolute truth in history. But history does require that we be **self-conscious** in our study of man, unlike science which requires only the conscious study of nature. Collingwood asks one question of history: what is the manner and meaning of its search? Does it provide us with information, derived empirically, that is designed to answer man's need to know himself?

Alan Bullock accepts that history is an intellectual discipline subject to the rules of evidence, but finds it more to the point to compare the historian with the painter and the novelist. Those historians who have taken the substance of science for their example in an effort to create generalizations of an abstract nature have no doubt misunderstood science and history alike. It may be true that science has functioned comfortably in taking abstractions for concrete reality. History can never do the same. It is the particular person or event, in unique circumstances, that normally fascinates the historian, calling forth all the finesse he can muster to narrate his tale. Bullock concludes: "it is a fair question to ask—who sees the more—the airman who flies continually across several countries five thousand feet up, from where he can see the land for miles and miles, or the countryman who has lived in one place all his life but knows the valleys, the woods and lanes of his own countryside like the back of his hand?"

Henri Pirenne would doubtless embrace Bullock's thesis that history is humane, but he has broadened it to call for a universal history based on the historian's widest experience. A truly universal humanism allows us to ask those questions that history is suitably equipped to answer. In so answering we would still be bound by science's way of proceeding—establishing the facts and then subjecting them to analysis, in order to provide ourselves with a satisfying explanation; or to echo Collingwood: we need first to discover what the document tells us, then what its author assumed he need not mention, and finally what its implications are for the critical thinker. It is at this point that Carl Becker's article is relevant, for he raises questions about the very nature of the fact with which we start.

In answer to the questions, what, where, and when is the historical fact, Becker answers: the historical fact is a symbol, or generalization if you will, to be found in the historian's mind, at the present time. An "implication follows from this. It is that the historian cannot eliminate the personal equation. Of course, no one can; not even, I think, the natural scientist. The universe speaks to us only in response to our purposes." Inasmuch as our purposes change, we can expect each man and each generation to write the same history anew. Hence historical knowledge is contingent upon man. Its excellence is a measure only of man's own excellence.

The humanism of history is endorsed by Isaiah Berlin's article in which he argues that the business of scientists is to devise general theories whereas the business of the historian is to attend to particularities. The use of causality in history, moreover, is based not on inductive or deductive logic, but on an understanding of ordinary human behavior. The better historian is likely to possess a capacity for sympathetic imagination that is rarely required of the scientist. This seemingly obvious difference between science and the humanities still remains obscure to many people although the distinction is at least as old as Blaise Pascal, who in the seventeenth century contrasted the geometrical spirit with the spirit of finesse or intuition. "In the intuitive mind the principles are found in common use, and are before the eyes of everybody. One has only to look; . . . it is only a question of good eyesight, but it must be good, for the principles are so subtle and so numerous that it is almost impossible but that some escape notice. . . . It is rare that mathematicians are intuitive . . . mathematicians wish to treat matters of intuition mathematically, and make themselves ridiculous, wishing to begin with definitions and then with axioms, which is not the way to proceed in intuitive reasoning. . . . The mathematical intellect has force and exactness, the intuitive intellect has comprehension." Such comprehension as distinct from mere apprehension is what the good historian forever seeks. The reasoning we employ may be the same for science and history alike, but the two subjects we reason about require and as well shape two different kinds of experience—of nature and of man. It has been history's mission to provide one of the surest avenues into the world of human experience.

ALAN BULLOCK

The Historian's Purpose:
History and Metahistory

Since Hegel delivered his lectures on the Philosophy of History in Berlin, he has had many imitators. Not that Hegel was the first to make the attempt at reading the meaning of history, but since his time historical prophecy has established its own apostolic succession from Hegel himself and Marx to Spengler and Wells, Croce and Toynbee. These interpretations are various and contradictory, but they have this in common: they are all attempts to discover in history patterns, regularities and similarities on whose recurrence is built a philosophical explanation of human existence, or at the very least a panoramic view of the stages of its development. It is this sort of *Weltanschauung*—metahistory, to borrow a phrase of Mr. Isaiah Berlin's—which is the fascination and justification of historical study to many people.

Equally obviously, it is not what most historians themselves mean by history. On the contrary, this is a kind of speculative activity which many professional historians eye with distrust and dislike. . . .

The commonest explanation for the hostility of many professional historians towards philosophical history in the grand style is

From Alan Bullock, "The Historian's Purpose: History and Metahistory," in *History Today,* vol. 7 (February, 1951), pp. 5–6, 8, 9–11.

to put it down to what Carlyle called "the poor, peddling dilettantism of Dryasdust," the contrast between the bold speculations of the philosopher of history and the narrow-mindedness of bloodless academic minds. But not all historians have been pedants or lacking in imagination. Is it true that the historian is confronted with a simple choice between metahistory on the model of Spengler or Toynbee and the desolate wastes of an arid historical erudition? Some historians at any rate—men like Halévy, Pirenne, Mathiez, Marc Bloch—seem to have found a way between these two extremes. . . . To borrow a quotation from Pirenne: "Without hypothesis or synthesis, history remains a pastime for antiquarians; just as without criticism and erudition it loses itself in the realm of fantasy."

Now, the moment the historian begins to explain, he is bound to make use of general propositions of all kinds—about human behaviour, about the effect of economic factors and the influence of ideas and a hundred other things. It is impossible for the historian to banish such general propositions; they are smuggled in by the back door, even when he refuses to admit it. He cannot begin to think or explain events without the help of the preconceptions, the assumptions, the generalization of experience which he brings with him—and is bound to bring with him—to his work . . . . For the historian such generalizations are hypotheses which he can use to open up a subject and suggest lines of approach, discarding, adapting, or continuing with them, as they prove fruitful. Few historians to-day, for instance, would fail to make use of the economic interpretation of history as one of the most valuable instruments of historical analysis—but only as one. As an experimental hypothesis, to be dropped or taken up as it fits, it is indispensable; as a dogmatic belief it cramps the mind and forces the historian to distort the evidence. It is in this way, as hypotheses, as the expression of probabilities, of what to look out for, that the historian treats his general proposition; not as the basis of something that can be built up into a general law. His purpose is not to form general propositions about revolutions or civilizations as such, but to give an account of the French or the Russian Revolution, to trace the rise and fall of the Hellenic or Chinese Civilizations.

In such work it is obvious that the first rule of the historian must be to keep a critical eye on his own assumptions and pre-conceptions, lest these should lead him to miss the importance of some piece of evidence, the existence of some connection. His whole training teaches him to break down rather than build up generalizations, to bring the general always to the touchstone of particular, concrete instances. His experience of this discipline and its results makes him cautious and sceptical about the possibility of establishing uniformities and regularities of sufficient generality to bear the weight of the conclusions then built up on them. Probabilities, yes—rules of thumb, the sort of thing you can expect to happen—but not more than this . . . . It is too easily assumed that the only approach to knowledge and understanding of human life and behaviour is by the search for general factors, regularities and uniformities, which can be reduced to formulas and general propositions. This is not a popular objection to raise. I can still remember the look of horror on the face of a young sociologist when I suggested there was more to be learned from Dostoievski's novels or Shakespeare's plays, with their series of individual portraits, than from the abstract and meagre generalizations of his own study. In that preference for the concrete and the particular, that distrust of the abstract and general which is the characteristic of many historians, there may be something akin to the approach of the painter and the novelist—think of Proust, for instance, and his incomparable re-creation of the past.

Probably it is a question of temperament, of the way your mind works. But behind the historian's distrust of the metahistorians and the dogmatists there often lies an instinctive feeling that, alongside the approach to knowledge of human nature and human behaviour represented by the attempt to frame general laws and trace broad general patterns of historical development, there is another approach, equally legitimate and to some people's way of thinking more fruitful. That is, by studying and trying to penetrate in all its individuality and uniqueness the development of one society, or one civilization, the behaviour not of men and women in general, but of one particular group in a given period of time. And it is a fair question to ask—who sees the more—the airman who flies continually across several countries five thousand feet up, from where he can see the land for miles and miles, or the countryman who has lived in one place all his life but knows the valleys, the woods and lanes of his own countryside like the back of his hand?

HENRI PIRENNE

What Are Historians Trying to Do?

Historical construction, the utilization of facts, is the inevitable result of all the processes of criticism that we have rapidly reviewed. They have meaning and value only through it; they are only the means to the end.

To construct history is to narrate it. From its first existence it has consisted in narratives, that is, the telling of a succession of related episodes. Indeed, the essential work of the historian is to bring these episodes to light, to show the relations existing between events, and in relating to explain them. Thus it appears that history is the expository narration of the course of human societies in the past.

All historical narrative is at once a synthesis and a hypothesis. It is a synthesis insomuch as it combines the mass of known facts in an account of the whole; it is a hypothesis insomuch as the relations that it establishes between these facts are neither evident nor verifiable by themselves. To unite the facts into an ensemble and relate them is in practice one and the same process. For it goes without saying that the grouping of facts will differ according to the idea one wants to give of their relation. Everything then depends upon this—as we are about to see—and upon the degree of creative imagination of the historians and upon his general conception of human affairs. This amounts to saying that in its highest and most essential expression history is a conjectural science, or, in other words, a subjective science.

This does not mean that it is at the mercy of fantasy and arbitrary procedures. It proceeds according to a method, but according to a method which its very subject obliges it to renew constantly. The historian is no less critical in making use of facts than in the study of sources, but the complexity of his task forces him here to have recourse in a much larger measure to conjecture.

All historical construction—which amounts to saying all historical narrative—rests upon a postulate: that of the eternal identity of human nature. One cannot comprehend men's actions at all unless one assumes in the beginning that their physical and moral beings have been at all periods what they are today. Past societies would remain unintelligible to us if the natural needs which they experienced and the psychical forces which stimulated them were qualitatively different from ours. How are the innumerable differences that humanity presents in time and space to be explained if one does not consider them as changing nuances of a reality which is in its essence always and everywhere the same?

The historian assumes, therefore, that he can treat the actions of the dead as he does those of the living who surround him. And this comparison suffices to make comprehensible the subjective element in his accounts. For to reason about men's actions is to trace them back to their motives and to attribute consequences to them. But where are these motives and consequences to be found if not in the mind of him who does the reasoning? Observers differ not only according to variations in intelligence but also in the depth and the variety of their knowledge. It is by intelligence that Thucydides is a greater historian than Xenophon, and Machiavelli than Froissart. But it is by the extent of knowledge that modern historians have the advantage over those of antiquity and the Middle Ages. They doubtless do not surpass their predecessors in point of vigor and penetration of mind; but by the variety of their knowledge they discover relationships between men's acts which have escaped the former.

For long centuries the destinies of societies were explained only by the intervention of some deity and the influence of great men. History appeared essentially as drama. Farsighted minds, Polybius, for example, perceived the importance of institutions in the activity of the state. But taken all in all, history, even in the case of the most eminent authors, was only the narration and the explanation of political events. The advance of the moral and social sciences has made the narrowness and insufficiency of this conception apparent. What these sciences teach us about all sorts of factors—religious, ethnic, geographic, economic—which have determined the development of societies at various epochs, has necessarily contributed to the understanding of a mass of phenomena which formerly passed unnoticed. The knowledge of social relations being inordinately augmented, historians are in a position to discover between the facts of the past a multitude of relations which were never before taken into account. They consider the history of much more remote periods than were formerly included, and from their vantage point they discover infinitely more variation, fulness, and life. One can say with strict accuracy that with much less material at our disposal than Roman and Greek historians had, we know Greek and Roman history better than they did. We know it better and yet we are not in agreement about it at all, any more than we are about any other part of history.

To achieve certainty about a subject as flowing, diverse, and complex as social behavior is impossible. Each kind of activity reacts upon all others. How, then, distinguish in the ensemble the part taken by each? How evaluate exactly the role which, for example, the economic or the religious factor has played in a given evolution? The conditions indispensable to all really scientific knowledge—calculation and measurement—are completely lacking in this field. And the interference of chance and individuals increases still more the difficulty of the historian's task by constantly confronting him with the unforeseen, by changing at every moment the direction which events seemed to take.

Not to historical method but to the subjects with which history is concerned must be imputed the historians' want of precision and the fact that their results seem uncertain and contradictory. The human actions which they study cannot appear the same to different historians. It needs only a moment of reflection to understand that two historians using the same material will not treat it in an identical fashion, primarily because the creative imagination which permits them to single the factors of movements out of chaos varies, but also because they do not have the same ideas as to the relative importance of the motives which determine men's conduct. They will inevitably write accounts which will contrast as do their personalities, depending upon the relative value they place on individual action or on the influence of collective phenomena; and, among these, on the emphasis they place on the economic, the religious, the ethnic, or the political factor. To this first cause of divergence we must add others. Historians are not conditioned in various ways solely by inherited qualities; their milieu is also important. Their religion, nationality, and social class influence them more or less profoundly. And the same is true of the period in which they work. Each epoch has its needs and tendencies which demand the attention of students and lead them to concentrate on this or that problem.

Thus, historical syntheses depend to a very large degree not only upon the personality of their authors but upon all the social, religious, or national environments which surround them. It follows, therefore, that each historian will establish between the facts relationships determined by the convictions, the movements, and the prejudices that have molded his point of view. All historical narrative is, as we have said, a hypothesis. It is an attempt at explanation, a conjectural reconstitution of the past. Each author throws light on some part, brings certain features into relief, considers certain aspects. The more these accounts multiply, the more the infinite reality is freed from its veils. All these accounts are incomplete, all imperfect, but all contribute to the advancement of knowledge. Those whose results have passed out of date have served to elaborate others which are in their turn replaced. For, in order that history may progress, the parallel development of synthesis and source criticism is indispensable. Without criticism synthesis would be only a sterile play of the imagination, and criticism would be merely dead erudition if it did not continually enlarge the field of its investigation and open new roads by the problems which it raises and the conjectures to which it gives birth.

We must believe, moreover, that in the measure in which the field is enlarged the work of historians will be accomplished under more satisfactory conditions. Up to the present time it has touched only a very restricted part of the immense subject which concerns it. In the field of ancient history, Greece and Rome; and in more modern times, the various national histories have attracted the efforts of investigators almost exclusively. Only today have we begun to discover the Orient, and we know what a transformation has consequently taken place in our comprehension of ancient history. Hellenic and Roman genius, in the dim light of records coming from Crete, Syria, Babylon, and Egypt, appear today as results of contact and interpenetration among different civilizations.

The comparative method alone can diminish racial, political, and national prejudices among historians. These prejudices inevitably ensnare him who, confined within the narrow limits of national history, is condemned to understand it badly because he is incapable of comprehending the bonds attaching it to the histories of other nations. It is not due to *parti pris* but because of insufficient information that so many historians lack impartiality. One who is lost in admiration of his own people will inevitably exaggerate their originality and give them the honor for discoveries which are in reality only borrowed. He is unjust to others because he fails to understand them, and the exclusiveness of his knowledge lays him open to the deceptions of the idols set up by sentiment. The comparative method permits history to appear in its true perspective. What was believed to be a mountain is razed to the size of a molehill, and the thing for which national genius was honored is often revealed as a simple manifestation of the imitative spirit. But the point of view of comparative history is none other than that of universal history. Therefore to the degree in which history is viewed in the totality of its development, and in which one accustoms himself to study particular or national histories in the functioning of general evolution, will the weaknesses inherent in historical method be diminished. It will attain the maximum precision which its subject permits when the final goal is clearly perceived by its adepts to be the scientific elaboration of universal history.

CARL BECKER

What Are Historical Facts?

What then is the historical fact? Far be it from me to define so illusive and intangible a thing! But provisionally I will say this: the historian may be interested in anything that has to do with the life of man in the past—any act or event, any emotion which men have expressed, any idea, true or false, which they have entertained. Very well, the historian is interested in some event of this sort. Yet he cannot deal directly with this event itself, since the event itself has disappeared. What he can deal with directly is a *statement about the event*. He deals in short not with the event, but with a statement which affirms *the fact that the event occurred*. When we really get down to the hard facts, what the historian is always dealing with is an *affirmation*—an affirmation of the fact that something is true. There is thus a distinction of capital importance to be made: the distinction between the ephemeral event which disappears, and the affirmation about the event which persists. For all practical purposes it is this affirmation about the event that constitutes for us the historical fact. If so the historical fact is not the past event, but a symbol which

From Carl Becker, "What Are Historical Facts?" in *Western Political Quarterly,* vol. 8, no. 3 (September, 1955), pp. 330–340. Reprinted by permission of the University of Utah, copyright owners.

enables us to recreate it imaginatively. Of a symbol it is hardly worthwhile to say that it is cold or hard. It is dangerous to say even that it is true or false. The safest thing to say about a symbol is that it is more or less appropriate.

This brings me to the second question—Where is the historical fact? I will say at once, however brash it sounds, that the historical fact is in someone's mind or it is nowhere. To illustrate this statement I will take an event familiar to all. "Abraham Lincoln was assassinated in Ford's Theater in Washington on the 14th of April, 1865." That *was* an actual event, occurrence, fact at the moment of happening. But speaking now, in the year 1926, we say it *is* an historical fact. We don't say that it *was* an historical fact, for that would imply that it no longer is one. We say that it *was* an actual event, but *is now* an historical fact. The actual occurrence and the historical fact, however closely connected, are two different things. Very well, if the assassination of Lincoln is an historical fact, where is this fact now? Lincoln is not being assassinated now in Ford's Theater, or anywhere else (except perhaps in propagandist literature!). The actual occurrence, the event, has passed, is gone forever, never to be repeated, never to be again experienced or witnessed by any living person. Yet this is precisely the sort of thing the historian is concerned with—events, acts, thoughts, emotions that have forever vanished as actual occurences. How can the historian deal with vanished realities? He can deal with them because these vanished realities give place to pale reflections, impalpable images or ideas of themselves, and these pale reflections, and impalpable images which cannot be touched or handled are all that is left of the actual occurrence. These are therefore what the historian deals with. These are his "material." He has to be satisfied with these, for the very good reason that he has nothing else. Well then, where are they—these pale reflections and impalpable images of the actual? Where are these facts? They are, as I said before, in his mind, or in somebody's mind, or they are nowhere.

Ah, but they are in the records, in the sources, I hear someone say. Yes, in a sense, they are in the sources. The historical fact of Lincoln's assassination is in the records—in contemporary newspapers, letters, diaries, etc. In a sense the fact is there, but in what sense? The records are after all only paper, over the surface of which ink has been distributed in certain patterns. And even these patterns were not made by the actual occurrence, the assassination of Lincoln. The patterns are themselves only "histories" of the event, made by someone who had in *his* mind an image or idea of Lincoln's assassination. Of course we, you and I, can, by looking at these inky patterns, form in *our* minds images or ideas more or less like those in the mind of the person who made the patterns. But if there were now no one in the world who could make any meaning out of the patterned records or sources, the fact of Lincoln's assassination would cease to be an historical fact. You might perhaps call it a dead fact; but a fact which is not only dead, but not known ever to have been alive, or even known to be now dead, is surely not much of a fact. At all events, the historical facts lying dead in the records can do nothing good or evil in the world. They become historical facts, capable of doing work, of making a difference, only when someone, you or I, bring them alive in our minds by means of pictures, images, or ideas of the actual occurrence. For this reason I say that the historical fact is in someone's mind, or it is nowhere, because when it is in no one's mind it lies in the records inert, incapable of making a difference in the world.

But perhaps you will say that the assassination of Lincoln has made a difference in the world, and that this difference is now effectively working, even if, for a moment, or an hour or a week, no one in the world has the image of the actual occurrence in mind. Quite obviously so, but why? Quite obviously because after the actual event people remembered it, and because ever since they have continued to remember it, repeatedly forming images of it in their mind. If the people of the United States had been incapable of enduring memory, for example, like dogs (as I assume; not being a dog I can't be sure) would the assassination of Lincoln be now doing work in the world, making a difference? If everyone had forgotten the occurrence after forty-eight hours, what difference would the occurrence have made, then or since? It is precisely because people have long memories, and have constantly formed images in their minds of the assassination of Lincoln, that the universe contains the historical fact which persists as well as the actual event which does not persist. It is the persisting historical fact, rather than the ephemeral actual event, which makes a difference to us now; and the historical fact makes a difference only because it is, and so far as it is, in human minds.

Now for the third question—When is the historical fact? If you agree with what has been said (which is extremely doubtful) the answer seems simple enough. If the historical fact is present, imaginatively, in someone's mind, then it is now, a part of the present. But the word present is a slippery word, and the thing itself is worse than the word. The present is an indefinable point in time, gone before you can think it; the image or idea which I have now present in mind slips instantly into the past. But images or ideas of past events are often, perhaps always, inseparable from images or ideas of the future. Take an illustration. I awake this morning, and among the things my memory drags in to enlighten or distress me is a vague notion that there was something I needed particularly to remember but cannot—a common experience surely. What is it that I needed to remember I cannot recall; but I can recall that I made a note of it in order to jog my memory. So I consult my little pocket memorandum book—a little Private Record Office which I carry about, filled with historical sources. I take out my memorandum book in order to do a little historical research; and there I find (Vol. I, p. 20) the dead historical fact—"Pay Smith's coal bill today: $1,016." The image of the memorandum book now drops out of mind, and is replaced by another image—an image of what? Why an image, an idea, a picture (call it what you will) made up of three things more or less inseparable. First the image of myself ordering coal from Smith last summer; second, the image of myself holding the idea in mind that I must pay the bill; third, the image of myself going down to Smith's office at four o'clock to pay it. The image is partly of things done in the past, and partly of things to be done in the future; but it is more or less all one image now present in mind.

Someone may ask, "Are you talking of history or of the ordinary ills of every day that men are heir to?" Well, perhaps Smith's coal bill is only my personal affair, of no concern to anyone else, except Smith to be sure. Take then another example. I am thinking of the Congress of Berlin, and that is without doubt history—the real thing. The historical facts of the Congress of Berlin I bring alive in memory, imaginatively. But I am making an image of the Congress of Berlin for a purpose; and indeed without a purpose no one would take the trouble to bring historical facts to mind. My purpose happens to be to convey this image of the Congress of Berlin to my class in History 42, in Room C, tomorrow afternoon at 3 o'clock. Now I find that inseparable from this image of the Congress of Berlin, which occurred in the past, are flitting images of myself conveying this image of the Congress of Berlin to my class tomorrow in Room C. I picture myself standing there monotonously talking, I hear the labored sentences painfully issuing forth, I picture the students' faces alert or bored as the case may be; so that images of this future event enter into the imagined picture of the Congress of Berlin, a past event; enter into it, coloring and shaping it too, to the end that the performance may do credit to me, or be intelligible to immature minds, or be compressed within the limits of fifty minutes, or to accomplish some other desired end. Well, this living historical fact, this mixed image of the coal bill or the Congress of Berlin— is it past, present, or future? I cannot say. Perhaps it moves with the velocity of light, and is timeless. At all events it is real history to me, which I hope to make convincing and real to Smith, or to the class in Room C.

I have now asked my three questions, and have made some remarks about them all. I don't know whether these remarks will strike you as quite beside the mark, or as merely obvious, or as novel. If there is any novelty in them, it arises, I think, from our inveterate habit of thinking of the world of history as part of the external world, and of historical facts as actual events. In truth the actual past is gone; and the world of history is an intangible world, re-created imaginatively, and present in our minds. If, as I think, this is true, then there are certain important implications growing out of it; and if you are not already exhausted I should like to touch upon a few of these implications. I will present them "firstly," "secondly," and so on, like the points of a sermon, without any attempt at coordination.

One implication is that by no possibility can the historian present in its entirety any actual event, even the simplest. You may think this a commonplace, and I do too; but still it needs to be often repeated because one of the fondest illusions of nineteenth century historians was that the historian, the "scientific" historian, would do just that: he would "present all the facts and let them speak for themselves." The historian would contribute nothing himself, except the sensitive plate of his mind, upon which the objective facts would register their own unimpeachable meaning. Nietzsche has described the nineteenth-century "objective man" with the acid precision of his inimitable phrases.

> The objective man is in truth a mirror. Accustomed to prostrating himself before something that wishes to be known, with such desires only as knowing implies, he waits until something comes and then expands himself sensitively, so that even the light footsteps and gliding past of spiritual beings may not be lost on his surface and film. Whatever personality he still possesses seems to him—disturbing; so much has he come to regard himself as the reflection of outward forms and events. Should one wish love and hatred from him, he will do what he can, and furnish what he can. But one must not be surprised if it should not be much. His mirroring and eternally self-polishing soul no longer knows how to affirm, no longer how to deny. . . . He is an instrument, but nothing in himself—*presque rien!*

The classical expression of this notion of the historian as instrument, is the famous statement attributed to Fustel de Coulanges. Half a century ago the French mind was reacting strongly against the romantic idea that political liberty was brought into Gaul by the primitive Germans; and Fustel was a leader in this reaction. One day he was lecturing to his students on early French institutions, and suddenly they broke into applause. "Gentlemen," said Fustel, "do not applaud. It is not I who speak, but history that speaks through me." And all the time this calm disinterested historian was endeavoring, with concentrated purpose, to prove that the damned Germans had nothing to do with French civilization. That of course was why the students applauded—and why Fustel told them that it was history that was speaking.

Well, for twenty years I have taken it for granted that no one could longer believe so preposterous an idea. But the notion continues to bob up regularly; and only the other day, riding on the train to the meeting of the Historical Association, Mr. A. J. Beveridge, eminent and honored historian, assured me dogmatically (it would be dogmatically) that the historian has nothing to do but "present all the facts and let them speak for themselves." And so I repeat what I have been teaching for twenty years, that this notion is preposterous; first, because it is impossible to present all the facts; and second, because even if you could present all the facts the miserable things wouldn't say anything, would say just nothing at all.

Let us return to the simple fact: "Lincoln was assassinated in Ford's Theater, in Washington, April 14, 1865." This is not all the facts. It is, if you like, a *representation* of all the facts, and a representation that perhaps satisfies one historian. But another historian, for some reason, is not satisfied. He says: "On April 14, 1865, in Washington, Lincoln, sitting in a private box in Ford's Theater watching a play, was shot by John Wilkes Booth, who then jumped to the stage crying out, *'Sic semper tyrannis!'* " That is a true affirmation about the event also. It represents, if you like, all the facts too. But its form and content (one and the same thing in literary discourse) is different, because it contains more of the facts than the other. Well, the point is that any number of affirmations (an infinite number if the sources were sufficient) could be made about the actual event, all true, all representing the event, but some containing more and some less of the factual aspects of the total event. But by no possiblity can the historian make affirmations describing all of the facts—all of the acts, thoughts, emotions of all of the persons who contributed to the actual event in its entirety. One historian will therefore necessarily *choose* certain affirmations about the event, and relate them in a certain way, rejecting other affirmations and other ways of relating them. Another historian will necessarily make a different choice. Why? What is it that leads one historian to make, out of all the possible true affirmations about the given event, certain affirmations and not others? Why, the purpose he has in his mind will determine that. And so the purpose he has in mind will determine the precise meaning which he derives from the event. The event itself, the facts, do not say anything, do not impose any meaning. It is the historian who speaks, who imposes a meaning.

A second implication follows from this. It is that the historian cannot eliminate the personal equation. Of course, no one can; not even, I think, the natural scientist. The universe speaks to us only in response to our purposes; and even the most objective constructions, those, let us say, of the theoretical physicist, are not the sole possible constructions, but only such as are found most convenient for some human need or purpose. Nevertheless, the physicist can eliminate the personal equation to a greater extent, or at least in a different way, than the historian, because he deals, as the historian does not, with an external world directly. The physicist presides at the living event, the historian presides only at the inquest of its remains. If I were alone in the universe and gashed my finger on a sharp rock, I could never be certain that there was anything there but my consciousness of the rock and gashed finger. But if ten other men in precisely the same way gash their fingers on the same sharp rock, we can, by comparing impressions, infer that there is something there besides consciousness. There is an external world there. The physicist can gash his finger on the rock as many times as he likes, and get others to do it, until they are all certain of the facts. He can, as Eddington says, make pointer-readings of the behavior of the physical world as many times as he likes for a given phenomenon, until he and his colleagues are satisfied. When their minds all rest satisfied they have an explanation, what is called the truth. But suppose the physicist had to reach his conclusions from miscellaneous records, made by all sorts of people, of experiments that had been made in the past, each experiment made only once, and none of them capable of being repeated. The external world he would then have to deal with would be the records. That is the case of the historian. The only external world he has to deal with is the records. He can indeed look at the records as often as he likes, and he can get dozens of others to look at them: and some things, some "facts," can in this way be established and agreed upon, as, for example, the fact that the document known as the Declaration of Independence was voted on July 4, 1776. But the meaning and significance of this fact cannot be thus agreed upon, because the series of events in which it has a place cannot be enacted again and again, under varying conditions, in order to see what effect

the variations would have. The historian has to judge the significance of the series of events from the one single performance,
never to be repeated, and never, since the records are incomplete
and imperfect, capable of being fully known or fully affirmed.
Thus into the imagined facts and their meaning there enters the
personal equation. The history of any event is never precisely the
same thing to two different persons; and it is well known that
every generation writes the same history in a new way, and puts
upon it a new construction.

The reason why this is so—why the same series of vanished
events is differently imagined in each succeeding generation—is
that our imagined picture of the actual event is always determined
by two things: (1) by the actual event itself insofar as we can
know something about it; and (2) by our own present purposes,
desires, prepossessions, and prejudices, all of which enter into the
process of knowing it. The actual event contributes something to
the imagined picture; but the mind that holds the imagined picture always contributes something too. This is why there is no
more fascinating or illuminating phase of history than historiography—the history of history: the history, that is, of what successive
generations have imagined the past to be like. It is impossible to
understand the history of certain great events without knowing
what the actors in those events themselves thought about history.
For example, it helps immensely to understand why the leaders of
the American and French Revolutions acted and thought as they
did if we know what their idea of classical history was. They
desired, to put it simply, to be virtuous republicans, and to act the
part. Well, they were able to act the part of virtuous republicans
much more effectively because they carried around in their heads
an idea, or ideal if you prefer, of Greek republicanism and
Roman virtue. But of course their own desire to be virtuous
republicans had a great influence in making them think the Greek
and Romans, whom they had been taught to admire by reading
the classics in school, were virtuous republicans too. Their image
of the present and future and their image of the classical past
were inseparable, bound together—were really one and the same
thing.

In this way the present influences our idea of the past, and our idea of the past influences the present. We are accustomed to say that "the present is the product of all the past"; and this is what is ordinarily meant by the historian's doctrine of "historical continuity." But it is only a half truth. It is equally true, and no mere paradox, to say that the past (our imagined picture of it) is the product of all the present. We build our conceptions of history partly out of our present needs and purposes. The past is a kind of screen upon which we project our vision of the future; and it is indeed a moving picture, borrowing much of its form and color from our fears and aspirations. The doctrine of historical continuity is badly in need of overhauling in the light of these suggestions; for that doctrine was itself one of those pictures which the early nineteenth century threw upon the screen of the past in order to quiet its deep-seated fears—fears occasioned by the French Revolution and the Napoleonic wars.

A third implication is that no one can profit by historical research, or not much, unless he does some for himself. Historical knowledge, however richly stored in books or in the minds of professors of history, is no good to me unless I have some of it. In this respect, historical research differs profoundly from research in the natural sciences, at least in some of them. For example, I know no physics, but I profit from physical researches every night by the simple act of pressing an electric light button. And everyone can profit in this way from researches in physics without knowing any physics, without knowing even that there is such a thing as physics. But with history it is different. Henry Ford, for example, can't profit from all the historical researches of two thousand years, because he knows so little history himself. By no pressing of any button can he flood the spare rooms of his mind with the light of human experience.

A fourth implication is more important than the others. It is that every normal person does know some history, a good deal in fact. Of course we often hear someone say: "I don't know any history; I wish I knew some history; I must improve my mind by learning some history." We know what is meant. This person means that he has never read any history books, or studied history in college; and so he thinks he knows no history. But it is precisely this conventional notion of history as something external to us, as a body of dull knowledge locked up in books, that obscures its real meaning. For, I repeat (it will bear repeating) every normal person—every man, woman, child—does know some history, enough for his immediate purposes; otherwise he would be a lost soul indeed. I suppose myself, for example, to have awakened this morning with loss of memory. I am all right otherwise; but I can't remember anything that happened in the past. What is the result? The result is that I don't know who I am, where I am, where to go, or what to do. I can't attend to my duties at the university, I can't read this paper before the Research Club. In short, my present would be unintelligible and my future meaningless. Why? Why, because I had suddenly ceased to know any history. What happens when I wake up in the morning is that my memory reaches out into the past and gathers together those images of past events, of objects seen, of words spoken and of thoughts thought in the past, which are necessary to give me an ordered world to live in, necessary to orient me in my personal world. Well, this collection of images and ideas of things past is history, my command of living history, a series of images of the past which shifts and reforms at every moment of the day in response to the exigencies of my daily living. Every man has a knowledge of history in this sense, which is the only vital sense in which he can have a knowledge of history. Every man has some knowledge of past events, more or less accurate; knowledge enough, and accurate enough, for his purposes, or what he regards as such. How much and how accurate, will depend on the man and his purposes. Now, the point is that history in the formal sense, history as we commonly think of it, is only an extension of memory. Knowledge or history, insofar as it is living history and not dead knowledge locked up in notebooks, is only an enrichment of our minds with the multiplied images of events, places, peoples, ideas, emotions outside our personal experience, an enrichment of our experience by bringing into our minds memories of the experience of the community, the nation, the race. Its chief value, for the individual, is doubtless that it enables a man to orient himself in a larger world than the merely personal, has the effect for him of placing the petty and intolerable present in a longer perspective, thus enabling him to judge the acts and thoughts of men, his own included, on the basis of an experience less immediate and restricted.

A fifth implication is that the kind of history that has most influence upon the life of the community and the course of events is the history that common men carry around in their heads. It won't do to say that history has no influence upon the course of events because people refuse to read history books. Whether the general run of people read history books or not, they inevitably picture the past in some fashion or other, and this picture, however little it corresponds to the real past, helps to determine their ideas about politics and society. This is especially true in times of excitement, in critical times, in time of war above all. It is precisely in such times that they form (with the efficient help of official propaganda!) an idealized picture of the past, born of their emotions and desires working on fragmentary scraps of knowledge gathered, or rather flowing in upon them, from every conceivable source, reliable or not matters nothing. Doubtless the proper function of erudite historical research is to be forever correcting the common image of the past by bringing it to the test of reliable information. But the professional historian will never get his own chastened and corrected image of the past into common minds if no one reads his books. His books may be as solid as you like, but their social influence will be nil if people do not read them and not merely read them, but read them willingly and with understanding.

It is, indeed, not wholly the historian's fault that the mass of men will not read good history willingly and with understanding; but I think we should not be too complacent about it. The recent World War leaves us with little ground indeed for being complacent about anything; but certainly it furnishes us with no reason for supposing that historical research has much influence on the course of events. The nineteenth century is often called the age of Science, and it is often called the age of history. Both statements are correct enough. During the hundred years that passed between 1814 and 1914 an unprecedented and incredible amount of research was carried on, research into every field of history—minute, critical, exhaustive (and exhausting!) research. Our libraries are filled with this stored up knowledge of the past; and never before has there been at the disposal of society so much reliable knowledge of human experience. What influence has all this expert research had upon the social life of our time? Has it done anything to restrain the foolishness of politicians or to enhance the wisdom of statesmen? Has it done anything to enlighten the mass of the people, or to enable them to act with greater wisdom or in response to a more reasoned purpose? Very little surely, if anything. Certainly a hundred years of expert historical research did nothing to prevent the World War, the most futile exhibition of unreason, take it all in all, ever made by civilized society. Governments and peoples rushed into this war with undiminished stupidity, with unabated fanaticism, with unimpaired capacity for deceiving themselves and others. I do not say that historical research is to blame for the World War. I say that it had little or no influence upon it, one way or another.

It is interesting, although no necessary part of this paper, to contrast this negligible influence of historical research upon social life with the profound influence of scientific research. A hundred years of scientific research has transformed the conditions of life. How it has done this is known to all. By enabling men to control natural forces it has made life more comfortable and convenient, at least for the well-to-do. It has done much to prevent and cure disease, to alleviate pain and suffering. But its benefits are not unmixed. By accelerating the speed and pressure of life it has injected into it a nervous strain, a restlessness, a capacity for irritation and an impatience of restraint never before known. And this power which scientific research lays at the feet of society serves equally well all who can make use of it—the harbingers of death as well as of life. It was scientific research that made the war of 1914, which historical research did nothing to prevent, a world war. Because of scientific research it could be, and was, fought with more cruelty and ruthlessness, and on a grander scale, than any previous war; because of scientific research it became a systematic massed butchery such as no one had dreamed of, or supposed possible. I do not say that scientific research is to blame for the war; I say that it made it the ghastly thing it was, determined its extent and character. What I am pointing out is that scientific research has had a profound influence in changing the condition of modern life, whereas historical research has had at best only a negligible influence. Whether the profound influence of the one has been of more or less benefit to humanity than the negligible influence of the other, I am unable to determine. Doubtless both the joys and frustrations of modern life, including those of the scholarly activities, may be all accommodated and reconciled within that wonderful idea of Progress which we all like to acclaim—none more so, surely, than historians and scientists.

ISAIAH BERLIN

The Concept of Scientific History

A. History, according to Aristotle, is an account of what individual human beings have done and suffered. In a still wider sense, history is what historians do. Is history, then, a natural science, as, let us say, physics or biology or phychology are sciences? And if not, should it seek to be one? And if it fails to be one, what prevents it? Is this due to human error or impotence, or to the nature of the subject, or does the very problem rest on a confusion between the concept of history and that of natural science? These have been questions that have occupied the minds of both philosophers and philosophically minded historians at least since the beginning of the nineteenth century, when men became self-conscious about the purpose and logic of their intellectual activities. But two centuries before that, Descartes had already denied to history any claim to be a serious study. Those who accepted the validity of the Cartesian criterion of what constitutes rational method could (and did) ask how they could find the clear and simple elements of which historical judgments

From Sir Isaiah Berlin, "The Concept of Scientific History," in William H. Dray (ed.), *Philosophical Analysis and History* (New York: Harper & Row, 1966), pp. 5–17, 31–53. Copyright ©1960 by Wesleyan University. Reprinted from *History and Theory*, Volume I, Number 1, by permission of Wesleyan University Press.

were composed, and into which they could be analysed; where were the definitions, the logical transformation rules, the rules of inference, the rigorously deduced conclusions? While the accumulation of this confused amalgam of memories and travelers' tales, fables and chroniclers' stories, moral reflections and gossip, might be a harmless pastime, it was beneath the dignity of serious men seeking what alone is worth seeking—the discovery of the truth in accordance with the principles and rules which alone guarantee scientific validity.

Ever since this doctrine of what was and what was not a science was enunciated, those who have thought about the nature of historical studies have laboured under the stigma of the Cartesian condemnation. Some have tried to show that history could be made respectable by being assimilated to one of the natural sciences whose overwhelming success and prestige in the seventeenth and eighteenth centuries held out promise of rich fruit wherever their methods were applicable; others declared that history was indeed a science, but a science in some different sense, with its own methods and canons, no less exacting, perhaps, than those of the sciences of nature, but resting on foundations different from them; there were those who defiantly declared that history was indeed subjective, impressionistic, incapable of being made rigorous, a branch of literature, or an embodiment of a personal vision—or that of a class, a church, a nation—a form of self-expression which was, indeed, its pride and justification: it laid no claim to universal and eternal objectivity and preferred to be judged as an interpretation of the past in terms of the demands of the present, or a philosophy of life, not as a science. Still others have tried to draw distinctions between sociology, which was a true science, and history, which was an art or, perhaps, something altogether *sui generis,* neither a science nor an art, but a discipline with its own structure and purposes, misunderstood by those who tried to draw false analogies between it and other intellectual activities.

B. In any case, the logic of historical thought and the validity of its credentials are issues that do not preoccupy the minds of the leading logicians of our day. The reasons for this are not far to seek. Nevertheless it remains surprising that philosophers pay more attention to the logic of such natural sciences as mathematics and physics, which comparatively few of them know well at first hand, and neglect that of history and the other humane studies, with which in the course of their normal education they tend to be more familiar.

C. Be that as it may, it is not difficult to see why there has been a strong desire to regard history as a natural science. History purports to deal with facts. The most successful method of identifying, discovering and inferring facts is that of the natural sciences. This is the only region of human experience, at any rate in modern times, in which progress has indubitably been made. It is natural to wish to apply methods successful and authoritative in one sphere to another, where there is far less agreement among specialists. The whole trend of modern empiricism has tended towards such a view. History is an account of what men have done and of what has happened to them. Man is largely, some would say wholly, a three-dimensional object in space and time, subject to natural laws: his bodily wants can be studied empirically as those of other animals. Basic human needs for, say, food or shelter or procreation, and his other biological or physiological requirements, do not seem to have altered greatly through the millennia, and the laws of the interplay of these needs with one another and with the human environment can all in principle be studied by the methods of the biological and, perhaps, psychological sciences. This applies particularly to the results of man's collective activities unintended by the agent, which, as the Historical School has emphasized since the days of Bossuet and Vico, play a decisive part in influencing his life, and which can surely be explained in purely mechanistic terms as fields of force or causal or functional correlations of human action and other natural processes. If only we could find a series of natural laws connecting at one end, the biological and physiological states and processes of human beings, with, at the other, the equally observable patterns of their conduct—their social activities in the wider sense—and so establish a coherent system of regularities, deducible from a comparatively small number of general laws (as

Newton, it is held, had so triumphantly done in physics), we should have in our hands a science of human behaviour. Then we could perhaps afford to ignore, or at least treat as secondary, such intermediate phenomena as feelings, thoughts, volitions, of which men's lives seem to themselves to be largely composed, but which do not lend themselves easily to exact measurement. If these data could be regarded as by-products of other, scientifically observable and measurable, processes, then we could predict the publicly observable behaviour of men (what more can a science ask for?) without taking the vaguer and more elusive data of introspection into much account. This would constitute the natural sciences of psychology and sociology, predicted by the materialists of the French Enlightenment, particularly Condillac and Condorcet and their nineteenth century followers—Comte, Buckle, Spencer, Taine, and many a modern behaviourist, positivist, and "physicalist" since their day.

D. What kind of science would history constitute? The traditional division of the sciences is into the inductive and the deductive. Unless one claimed acquaintance with *a priori* propositions or rules, derived not from observation but from knowledge based on intuition or revelation, of the laws governing the behaviour of men and of their goals, or of the specific purposes of their creator—and few historians since the Middle Ages have openly professed to possess such knowledge—this science could not be wholly deductive. But is it then inductive? It is difficult or impossible to conduct large-scale experiments on human beings, and knowledge must therefore largely rest on observation. However, this disability has not prevented astronomy or geology from becoming flourishing sciences, and the mechanists of the eighteenth century confidently looked forward to a time when the application of the methods of the mathematical sciences to human affairs would explode such myths as those of revealed truths, the inner light, a personal deity, an immaterial soul, freedom of the will, and so forth; and so solve all social problems by means of a scientific sociology as clear, exact, and capable of predicting future behaviour as, to use Condorcet's phrase, the sciences that study the societies of bees or beavers. In the nineteenth century this claim came to be regarded as too sweeping and too extravagant. It became clear that the methods and concepts of the mechanists were not adequate for dealing with growth and change; the adoption of more complex vitalistic or evolutionary categories and models served to demarcate the procedures of the biological from those of the purely physical sciences; the former seemed clearly more appropriate to the behavior and development of human beings. In the twentieth century psychology has begun to assume the role that biology had played in the previous century, and its methods and discoveries with regard both to individuals and to groups have in their turn transformed our approach to history.

E. Why should history have had so long to wait to become a science? Buckle, who believed in the science of history more passionately, perhaps, than any man who ever lived, explained this very simply by the fact that historians were "inferior in mental power" to the mathematicians and physicists and chemists. He declared that those sciences advanced fastest which in the first instance attracted the attention of the cleverest men, and their successes naturally in their turn attracted other able heads into their services. In other words, if men as gifted as Galileo or Newton, or even Laplace or Faraday, had devoted themselves to dealing with the disordered mass of truth and falsehood that went by the name of history, they could soon have set it to rights and made a firmly built, clear, and fertile natural science of it.[1] This was a promise held out by those who were,

---

[1] "In regard to nature, events apparently the most irregular and capricious have been explained and have been shown to be in accordance with certain fixed and universal laws. This has been done because men of ability, and above all, men of patient, untiring thought, have studied natural events with the view of discovering their regularity: and if human events were subjected to a similar treatment, we have every right to expect similar results. . . . Whoever is at all acquainted with what has been done during the last two centuries, must be aware that every generation demonstrates some events to be regular and predictable, which the preceding generation had declared to be irregular and unpredictable: so that the marked tendency of advancing civilization is to strengthen our belief in the universality of order, of method, and of law. This being the case, it follows that if any facts, or class of facts, have not yet been reduced to order, we, so far from pronouncing

very understandably, hypnotised by the magnificent progress of the natural sciences of their day. Intelligent and sceptical thinkers like Taine and Renan in France, not to speak of really passionate positivists like Comte, and, in some of their writings, Engels and Plekhanov, profoundly believed in this prospect. Their hopes have scarcely been fulfilled. It may be profitable to ask why this is so.

F. Before an answer to this question is attempted, two further sources of the belief that history can, at least in principle be transformed into a natural science may be noted. The first is perhaps conveyed best by the metaphors that, at any rate since the nineteenth century, all educated men have tended to use. When we speak of rational as opposed to utopian policies, we tend to say of the latter that they ignore, or are defeated by, the "inexorable logic of the (historical) facts" or the "wheels of history" which it is idle to try to stay. We speak of the futility of defying the "forces of history," or the absurdity of efforts to "put the clock back" or to "restore the past." We speak of the youth, the maturity, the decay of peoples or cultures, of the ebb and flow of social movements, of the rise and fall of nations. Such language serves to convey the idea of an inexorably fixed time order—the "river of time" on which we float, and which we must willy-nilly accept; a moving stair which we have not created, but on which

them to be irreducible, should rather be guided by our experience of the past, and should admit the probability that what we now call inexplicable will at some future time be explained. This expectation of discovering regularity in the midst of confusion is so familiar to scientific men, that among the most eminent of them it becomes an article of faith; and if the same expectation is not generally found among historians, it must be ascribed partly to their being of inferior ability to the investigators of nature, and partly to the greater complexity of those social phenomena with which their studies are concerned. . . . The most celebrated historians are manifestly inferior to the most successful cultivators of physical science: no one having devoted himself to history who in point of intellect is at all to be compared with Kepler, Newton, or many other . . . [nevertheless] I entertain little doubt that before another century has elapsed, the chain of evidence will be complete, and it will be as rare to find an historian who denies the undeviating regularity of the moral world, as it now is to find a philosopher who denies the regularity of the material world." Henry Thomas Buckle, *History of Civilization in England,* vol. I, ch. I.

we are borne, obeying, as it were, some natural law governing the order and shape of events—in this case, events consisting of, or at any rate affecting, human lives, activities, and experiences. Metaphorical and misleading thought such uses of words can be, they are pointers to categories and concepts in terms of which we conceive the "stream of history," namely, as something possessing a certain objective pattern that we ignore at our peril. It is a short step from this to conclude that whatever has a pattern exhibits regularities capable of being expressed in laws; and the systematic interconnection of laws is the content of a natural science.

The second source of this belief lies deeper still. Patterns of growth, or of the march of events, can plausibly be represented as a succession of causes and affects, capable of being systematised by natural science. But sometimes we speak as if something more fundamental than empirical connections (which Idealist philosophers call "mechanical," or "external" or "mere brute conjunctions") give their unity to the aspects, or the successive phases, of the existence of the human race on earth. When we say, for instance, that it is absurd to blame Richelieu for not acting like Bismarck because it is obvious that Richelieu could not have acted like a man living in Germany in the nineteenth century; and that conversely Bismarck could not have done what Richelieu accomplished, because the seventeenth century had its own character, very different from the deeds, events, characteristics of the eighteenth century which it uniquely determined, and which in their turn uniquely determined those of the nineteenth; what we are then affirming is that this order is an objective order; that those who do not understand that what is possible in one age and situation may be wholly inconceivable in another, fail to understand something universal and fundamental about the only way in which social life, or the human mind, or economic growth, or some other sequence, not merely does, but can, or perhaps must, develop. Similarly, when we say that the proposition that *Hamlet* was written at the court of Genghis Khan in Outer Mongolia is not merely false but absurd; that if someone acquainted with the relevant facts seriously supposes that it could have been written at that time and in that place, he is not merely unusually ignorant or mistaken, but out of his mind; that *Hamlet* not merely was not, but could not have been, written there or then—that we can dismiss this hypothesis without discussion—what is it that entitles us to feel so certain? What kind of "could not" is this "could not"? Do we rule out propositions asserting possibilities of this kind as being false on scientific, that is, empirical-inductive grounds? It seems to me that we call them grotesque (and not merely implausible or false) because they conflict, not just with this or that fact or generalization which we accept, but with presuppositions which are entailed by our whole thinking about the world—the basic categories that govern such central concepts of our thought as man, society, history, development, growth, barbarism, maturity, civilization, and the like. These presuppositions may turn out to be false or misleading (as, for example, teleolgy or deism are considered to have been by positivists or atheists), but they are not refuted by experiment or empirical observation. They are destroyed or transformed by those changes in the total outlook of a man or a milieu or a culture which it is the hardest (and the most important) test of the histories of ideas (and, in the end, of history as such) to be able to explain. What is here involved is a deeply ingrained, widespread, long-lived *Weltanschauung*—the unquestioning (and not necessarily valid) assumption of one particular objective order of events or facts. Sometimes it is a vertical order—succession in time—which makes us realise that the events or institutions of, say, the fourteenth century, because they were what they were, of necessity (however we analyse this sort of necessity), and not just as a matter of fact—contingently— occurred earlier than those of the sixteenth, which were "shaped," that is, in some sense, determined (some would say caused) by them; so that anyone who tries to date the works of Shakespeare before those of Dante, or to omit the fifteenth century altogether, fitting the end of the fourteenth into the beginning of the sixteenth century without a break, can be convicted of suffering from a defect different in kind, not degree, from (and less remedial than) ignorance or lack of scientific method. At other times we conceive of the order as "horizontal"; that is, it underlies the perception of the interconnections between different aspects of the same stage of culture—the kinds of assumptions and categories that the anti-mechanistic German philosophers of culture, Herder and his disciples (and before them Vico) brought to light. It is this kind of awareness (the historical sense) that is said to enable us to perceive that a certain type of legal structure is "intimately connected" with, or is part of the same complex as, an economic activity, a moral outlook, a style of writing or of dancing or of worship; it is by means of this gift (whatever may be its nature) that we recognise various manifestations of the human spirit as "belonging to" this or that culture or nation or historical period, although these manifestations may be as different from one another as the way in which men form letters on paper from their system of land tenure. Without this faculty we should attach no sense to such social-historical notions as "the typical," or "the normal," or "the discordant," or "the anachronistic," and consequently we should be unable to conceive the history of an institution as an intelligible pattern, or attribute a work of art to its time and civilization and milieu, or indeed be able to understand or explain how one phase of a civilization "generates" or "determines" another. This sense of what remains identical or unitary in differences and in change (of which Idealist philosophers have made altogether too much) is also a dominant factor in giving us our sense of unalterable trends, of the "one-directional" flow of history. From this it is easy to pass to the far more questionable belief that whatever is unalterable is so only because it obeys laws, and that whatever obeys laws can always be systematized into a science.

G. These are among the many factors that have made men crave for a natural science of history. All seemed ready, particularly in the nineteenth century, for the formulation of this new, powerful, and illuminating discipline, which would do away with the chaotic accumulation of facts, conjectures, and rules of thumb that had been treated with such disdain by Descartes and his scientifically-minded successors. The stage was set, but virtually nothing materialized. No general laws were formulated—nor even moderately reliable maxims—from which historians could deduce (together with knowledge of the initial conditions) either what would happen next, or what had happened in the past. The great machine which was to rescue them from the tedious labours of adding fact to fact and of attempting to construct a coherent account out of their hand-picked material, seemed like a plan in the head of a cracked inventor. The immense labour-saving instrument which, when fed with information, would itself order it, deduce the right conclusions, and offer the proper explanations, removing the need for the uncertain, old-fashioned, hand-operated tools with which historians had fumbled their way in the unregenerate past, remained a bogus prospectus, the child of an extravagant imagination, like designs for a perpetual motion machine. Neither psychologists nor sociologists, neither the ambitious Comte nor the more modest Wundt, had been able to create the new mechanism: the "nomothetic" sciences—the system of laws and rules under which the factual material could be ordered so as to yield new knowledge—remained stillborn.

One of the criteria of a natural science is rightly regarded as being its capacity for prediction; or, in the case of an historical study, retrodiction—filling in gaps in the past for which no direct testimony exists with the aid of extrapolation performed according to relevant rules or laws. A method of this conjectural sort is employed in archaeology or palaeontology where vast gaps in knowledge exist and there is no better—more dependable— avenue to factual truth in the absence of concrete factual evidence. In archaeology we make efforts to link our knowledge of one remote period to our knowledge of another by trying to reconstruct what must, or at least may have, occurred to account for the transition from one stage to the other through many unknown intermediate phases. But this way of filling gaps is commonly regarded as a none too reliable method of discovery of the past, and one to which no one would wish to resort if he could find the more concrete kind of evidence (however the quality and extent of such concreteness is assessed) on which we base knowledge of the historical, as opposed to prehistoric, period of human life; still less as a "scientific" substitute for it.

H. What would the structure of such a science be like, supposing that one were able to formulate it? It would, presumably, consist of causal or functional correlations—a system of interrelated general propositions of the type "whenever or wherever x

then or there *y"*—variables into which precise dates and places could be fitted; and it would possess two forms: the "pure" and the "applied." The "pure" sciences of social statics or social dynamics, of which Herbert Spencer perhaps a little too optimistically proclaimed the existence, would then be related to the "applied" science of history, somewhat as physics is to mechanics, or at least as anatomy applies to the diagnosis of specific cases by a physician. If it existed, such a science would have revolutionised the old empirical, hand-woven history by mechanising it, as astronomy abolished the rules of thumb accumulated by Babylonian stargazers, or as Newtonian physics transformed older cosmologies. No such science exists. Before we ask why this is so, it would perhaps be profitable to consider some of the more obvious ways in which history, as it has been written until our day, differs from a natural science conceived in this fashion.

I. Let me begin by noting one conspicuous difference between history and the natural sciences. Whereas in a developed natural science we consider it more rational to put our confidence in general propositions or laws than in specific phenomena (indeed this is part of the definition of rationality), this rule does not seem to operate successfully in history. Let me give the simplest possible kind of example. One of the common-sense generalisations that we regard as most firmly established is that the normal inhabitants of this planet can see the sun rise every morning. Suppose a man were to say that on a given morning he had not, despite repeated attempts, seen the sun rise; and that since one negative instance is, by the rules of our ordinary logic, sufficient to kill a general proposition, he regarded his carefully carried out observation as fatal not merely to the hitherto accepted generalisation about the succession of night and day, but to the entire system of celestial mechanics, and, indeed, of physics, which purports to reveal the causes of this phenomenon. This startling claim would not normally be regarded as a conclusion to be unhesitatingly accepted. Our first reaction would be to try to construct an *ad hoc* hypothesis to save our system of physics, supported as it is by the most systematic accumulation of controlled observation and deductive reasoning made by men. We should suggest to the objector that perhaps he was not looking at the right portion of the sky; that clouds intervened; that he was distracted; that his eyes were closed; that he was asleep; that he was suffering from an hallucination; that he was using words in unfamiliar senses; that he was lying or joking or insane; we should advance other explanations, any one of which would be compatible with his statement, and yet preserve physical science intact. It would not be rational to jump to the immediate conclusion that if the man, in our considered judgment, had told the truth, the whole of our hard-won physics must be rejected, or even modified. No doubt, if the phenomenon repeated itself, and other men failed to perceive the sun rise under normal conditions, some physical hypotheses, or indeed laws, might have to be drastically altered, or even rejected; perhaps the foundations of our physical sciences would have to be built anew. But we should only embark on this in the last resort. Yet if *per contra* an historian were to attempt to cast doubt on—or explain away— some piece of individual observation of a type not otherwise suspect, say, that Napoleon had been seen in a three-cornered hat at a given moment during the battle of Austerlitz; and if the historian did so solely because he put his faith, for whatever reason, in a theory or law according to which French generals or heads of state never wore three-cornered hats during battles, his method, one can safely assert, would not meet with universal or immediate recognition from his profession. Any procedure designed to discredit the testimony of normally reliable witnesses, or documents as, let us say, lies or forgeries, or as being defective at the very point at which the report about Napoleon's hat occurred, would be liable to be regarded as itself suspect, as an attempt to alter the facts to fit a theory. I have chosen a crude and trivial instance; it would not be difficult to think of more sophisticated examples, where an historian lays himself open to the charge of trying to press the facts into the service of a particular theory. Such historians are accused of being prisoners of their theories; they are accused of being fanatical or cranky or doctrinaire, of misrepresenting or misreading reality to fit in with their obsessions, and the like. Addiction to theory—being doctrinaire—is a term of abuse when applied to historians; it is not an insult if applied to a natural scientist. We are saying nothing derogatory if we say of a natural scientist that he is in the grip of a theory. We may complain if we think that his theory is false, or that he is ignoring relevant evidence, but we do not deplore the fact that he is trying to fit the facts into the pattern of a theory; for that is his business. It is the business of a natural scientist to be a theorist; that is, to formulate doctrines—true rather than false, but above all, doctrines; for natural science is nothing if it is not a systematic interlacing of theories and doctrines, built up inductively, or by hypothetical deductive methods, or whatever other method is considered best (logically reputable, rational, publicly testable, fruitful) by the most competent practitioners in the field. It seems clear that whereas in history we tend, more often than not, to attach greater credence to the existence of particular facts than to general hypotheses, however well supported, from which these facts could in theory be deduced, in a natural science the opposite seems more often to be the case: there it is (in cases of conflict) often more rational to rely upon a properly supported general theory—say, that of gravitation—than on particular observations. This difference alone, whatever its root, must cast *prima facie* doubt upon any attempt to draw too close an analogy between the methods of history and those of natural science. . . .

P. All this may be no more than another way of saying something trite but true—that the business of a science is to concentrate on similarities, not differences, to be general, to omit whatever is not relevant to answering the severely delimited questions that it sets itself to ask; while those historians who are concerned with a field wider than the specialized activities of men, are interested at least as much in the opposite—in that which differentiates one thing, person, situation, age, pattern of experience, individual or collective, from another. When such historians attempt to account for and explain, say, the French Revolution, the last thing that they seek to do is to concentrate only on those characteristics which the French Revolution has in common with other revolutions, to abstract only common recurrent characteristics, to formulate a law on the basis of them, or at any rate an hypothesis, from which something about the pattern of all revolutions as such (or, more modestly, all European revolutions) and therefore of this revolution in particular, could in principle be reliably inferred. This, if it were feasible, would be the task of sociology, which would then stand to history as a "pure" science to its application. The validity of the claim of this type of sociology to the status of a natural science is another story, and not directly related to history, whose tasks are different. The immediate purpose of narrative historians (as has often been repeated) whatever else it may be besides this, is to paint a portrait of a situation or a process, which, like all portraits, seeks to capture the unique pattern and peculiar characteristics of its particular subject; not to be an X-ray which eliminates all but what a great many subjects have in common. This is, by now, a truism, but its bearing on the possibility of transforming history into a natural science has not always been clearly perceived. Two great thinkers understood this, and grappled with the problem: Leibniz and Hegel. Both made heroic efforts to bridge the gulf by such doctrines as those of "individual essences" and "concrete universals"— a desperate dialectical attempt to fuse together individuality and universality. The imaginative brilliance of the metaphysical constructions in which the passage of the Rubicon is deducible from the essence of Julius Caesar, or the even more ambitious inevitabilities of the *Phenomenology,* and their failure, serves to indicate the central character of the problem.

Q. One way of appreciating this contrast is by contrasting two uses of the humble word "because." Max Weber, whose discussion of this problem is extraordinarily illuminating, asked himself under what conditions I accept an explanation of a given individual action or attitude as adequate, and whether these conditions are the same as those that are required in the natural sciences— that is to say, he tried to analyse what is meant by rational explanation in these contrasted fields. If I understand him correctly, the type of argument he uses goes somewhat as follows: Supposing that a doctor informs me that his patient recovered from pneumonia because he was injected with penicillin, what rational grounds have I for accepting this "because?" My belief is rational only if I have rational grounds for believing the general proposition "penicillin is effective against pneumonia," a causal proposition established by experiment and observation, which there is no reason to accept unless, in fact, it has been arrived at by valid methods of scientific inference. No amount of general reflection would justify my accepting this general proposition (or its application in a given case) unless I know that it has been or could be experimentally verfied. The "because" in this case indicates a claim that a *de facto* correlation between penicillin and pneumonia has, in fact, been established. I may find this correlation surprising or I may not; this does not affect its reality: scientific investigation—the logic of which, we now think, is hypothetical-deductive—establishes its truth or probability; and that is the end of the matter. If, on the other hand, I am told, in the course of an historical narrative (or in a work of fiction, or ordinary life) that X resented the behaviour of Y, because X was weak and Y was arrogant and strong; or that X forgave the insult he had received from Y, because he was too fond of Y to feel aggrieved, and if, having accepted these "because" statements as adequate explanations of the behaviour of X and Y, I am then challenged to produce the general law which I am leaning on, consciously or not, to "cover" these cases, what would it be reasonable for me to reply? I may well produce something like "the weak often resent the arrogant and strong," or "human beings forgive insults from those they love." But supposing I am then asked what concrete evidence I have for the truth of these general propositions, what scientific experiments I or anyone else have performed to establish these generalizations, how many observed and tested cases they rest on—I may well be at a loss to answer. Even if I am able to cite examples from my own or others' experience of the attitude of the weak to the strong, or of the behaviour of persons capable of love and friendship, I may be scornfully told by a psychologist—or any other devotee of strict scientific method—that the number of instances I have produced is ludicrously insufficient to be adequate evidence for a generalization of such scope; that no respectable science would accept these few positive or negative instances which, moreover, have not been observed under scientific conditions, as a basis for serious claims to formulate laws; that such procedures are impressionistic, vague, prescientific, unworthy to be reckoned as ground for a scientific hypothesis. And I may further be told that what cannot enter a natural science cannot be called fully rational but only an approximation to it (an "explanation sketch"). Implicit in this approach is Descartes' criterion, the setting up of the methods of mathematics (or physics) as the standard for all rational thought. Nevertheless, the explanation that I have given in terms of the normal attitude of the weak to the strong, or of friends to one another, would, of course, be accepted by most rational beings (writers and readers of history among them) as an adequate explanation of the behaviour of a given individual in the relevant situation. This kind of explanation may not be admissible in a treatise on natural science, but in dealing with others, or describing their actions, we accept it as being both normal and reasonable; neither as inescapably shallow, or shamefully unexamined, or doubtful, nor as necessarily needing support from the laboratory. We may, of course, in any given case, be mistaken—mistaken about particular facts to be accounted for, about the attitudes of the relevant individuals to one another, or in taking for granted the generalizations implicit in our judgment; these may well be in need of correction from psychologists or sociologists. But because we may be in error in a given instance, it does not follow that this type of explanation is always systematically at fault, and should or could always be replaced by something more searching, more inductive, more like the type of evidence that is alone admitted in, say, biology. If we probe further and ask why it is that such explanations—such uses of "because"—are accepted in history, and what is meant by saying that it is rational to accept them, the answer must surely be that what in ordinary life we call adequate explanations often rest not on specific pieces of scientific reasoning, but on our experience in general, on our capacity for understanding of the habits of thought and action that are embodied in human attitudes and behaviour, on what is called knowledge of life, sense of reality. If someone tells us "X forgave Y because he loved him," or "X killed Y because he hated him," we accept these propositions easily, because they, and the propositions into which they can be generalized, fit in with our experience, because we claim to know what men are

like, not, as a rule, by careful observation of them as psychological specimens (as Taine recommends), or as members of some
strange tribe whose behaviour is obscure to us and can only be
inferred from (preferably controlled) observation, but because we
claim to know (not always justifiably) what—in essentials—a
human being is, in particular a human being who belongs to a
civilization not too unlike our own, and consequently one who
thinks, wills, feels, acts in a manner which (rightly or wrongly)
we assume to be intelligible to us because it sufficiently resembles
our own or those of other human beings whose lives are inter-
twined with our own. This sort of "because" is the "because"
neither of induction nor of deduction, but the "because" of understanding—*Verstehen*—of recognition of a given piece of behaviour as being part and parcel of a pattern of activity which we can
follow, which we can remember or imagine, and which we describe in terms of the general laws which cannot possibly all be
rendered explicit (still less organized into a system), but without
which the texture of normal human life—social or personal—is
not conceivable. We make mistakes; we may be shallow, unobser-
vant, naïve, unimaginative, not allow enough for unconscious
motives, or unintended consequences, or the play of chance or
some other factor; we may project the present into the past or
assume uncritically that the basic categories and concepts of our
civilization apply to remote or dissimilar cultures which they do
not fit. But although any one explanation or use of "because" and
"therefore" may be rejected or shaken for any of these or a
hundred reasons (which scientific discoveries in, say, physics or
psychology, running against the complacent assumptions of common sense may well provide), *all* such explanations cannot be
rejected *in toto* in favour of inductive procedures derived from the
natural sciences, because that would cut the ground from beneath
our feet: the context in which we think, act, expect to be understood or responded to, would be destroyed. When I understand a
sentence which someone utters, my claim to know what he means
is not, as a rule, based on an inductively reached conclusion that
the statistical probability that the noises he emits are, in fact,
related and expressive in the way that I take them to be—a
conclusion derived from a comparison of the sounds he utters with

a great many other sounds that a great many other beings have uttered in corresponding situations in the past. This must not be confused with the fact that, if pressed to justify my claim, I could conduct an experiment which would do something to support my belief. Nevertheless, my belief is usually a good deal stronger than that which any process of reasoning that I may perform with a view to bolstering it up would, in a natural science, be held to justify. Yet we do not for this reason regard such claims to understanding as being less rational than scientific convictions, still less as being arbitrary. When I say that I realize that X forgave Y because he loved him or was too good-natured to bear a grudge, what I am ultimately appealing to is my own (or my society's) experience and imagination, my (or my associates') knowledge of what such relationships have been and can be. This knowledge, whether it is my own, or taken by me on trust— accepted uncritically—may often be inadequate, and may lead me to commit blunders—a Freudian or a Marxist may open my eyes to much that I had not [understood]—but if *all* such knowledge were rejected unless it could pass scientific tests, I could not think or act at all.

R. The world of natural science is the world of the external observer noting as carefully and dispassionately as he can the compresence or succession (or lack of it), or the extent of correlation, of empirical characteristics. In formulating a scientific hypothesis, I must, at least in theory, start from the initial assumption that, for all I know, anything might occur next door to, or before or after, or simultaneously with, anything else; nature is full of surprises; I must take as little as possible for granted; it is the business of natural science to establish general laws recording what most often or invariably does occur. But in human affairs, in the interplay of men with one another, of their feelings, thoughts, choices, ideas about the world or each other or themselves, it would be absurd (and if pushed to extremes, impossible) to start in this manner. I do not start from an ignorance which leaves all doors—or as many of them as possible—open, for here I am not primarily an external observer, but myself an actor; I understand other human beings, and what it is to have motives, feelings, or follow rules, because I am human myself, and because to be active—that is, to want, intend, make plans, speculate, do, react to others self-consciously, be aware of my situation *vis-à-vis* other conscious beings and the non-human environment—is *eo ipso* to be engaged in a constant fitting of fragments of reality into the single all-embracing pattern that I assume to hold for others besides myself, and which I call reality. When, in fact, I am successful in this—when the fragments seem to me to fit—we call this an explanation; when in fact they do fit, I am called rational; if they fit badly, if my sense of harmony is largely a delusion, I am called irrational, fanciful, distraught, silly; if they do not fit at all, I am called mad.

S. So much for differences in method. But there is also a profound difference of aim between scientific and historical studies. What they seek for is not the same. Let me illustrate this with a simple example. Supposing that we look at an average, unsophisticated European or American school text of modern European history that offers a sample of the kind of elementary historical writing upon which most of us have been brought up. Let us consider the kind of account that one finds (or used to find) in routine works of this type, of, say, the causes of the French Revolution. It is not unusual to be told that among them were—to give the headings: (i) the oppression of French peasants by the aristocracy, the Church, the King, etc.; (ii) the disordered state of French finances; (iii) the weak character or the stupidity of Louis XVI; (iv) the subversive influence of the writings of Voltaire, the Encyclopaedists, Rousseau, and other writers; (v) the mounting frustration of the ambitions of the economically rising French *bourgeoisie,* barred from its proper share of political power; and so on. One may reasonably protest against the crudity and naïveté of such treatments of history: Tolstoy has provided some very savage and entertaining parodies of it and its practitioners. But if one's main anxiety is to convert history into a science, one's indignation should take a different and much more specific form. One should declare that what is here manifested is a grotesque confusion of categories, an outrage to scientific method. For the analysis of the condition of the peasants belongs to the science of economics, or perhaps of social history; that of French fiscal policy to the science of public finance, which is not primarily an historical study, but one founded (according to some) on timeless principles; the weakness of the King's character or intellect is a matter for individual psychology (or biography); the influence of Voltaire and Rousseau belongs to the history of ideas; the pressure of the middle classes is a sociological topic, and so forth. Each of these disciplines must surely possess its own factual content, methods, canons, concepts, categories, logical structure. To heap them into one, and reel off a list of causes, as if they all belonged to the same level and type, is intellectually scandalous: the rope composed of these wholly heterogeneous strands must at once be unwound; each of the strands must then be treated separately in its proper logical box. Such should be the reaction of someone who takes seriously the proposition that history is, or at any rate should be, a natural science or a combination of such sciences. Yet the truth about history—perhaps the most important truth of all—is that general history *is* precisely this amalgam, a rich brew composed of apparently disparate ingredients, that we do in fact think of these different causes as factors in a single unitary sequence—the history of the French nation or French society during a particular segment of time—and that although there may be great profit to be gained from detaching this or that element of a single process for analysis in a specialised laboratory, yet to treat as if they were genuinely separate, insulated streams which do not compose a single river, is a far wilder departure from what we think history to be, than the indiscriminate compounding of them into one string of causes, as is done in the simple-minded schoolbooks. "History is what historians do," and what at any rate some historians aim at is to answer those who wish to be told what important changes occurred in French public life between 1789 and 1794, and why they took place. We wish, ideally at least, to be presented, if not with a total experience—which is a logical as well as practical impossibility—at least with something full enough and concrete enough to meet our conception of public life (itself an abstraction, but not a deductive schema, not an artificially constructed model) seen from as many points of view and at as many levels as possible, including as many components, factors, aspects, as the widest and deepest knowledge, the greatest analytical power, insight, imagination, can present. If we are told that this cannot be achieved by a natural science—that is, by the application of models to reality, because models can only function if their subject matter is relatively "thin," consisting, as it does, of deliberately isolated strands of experience and not "thick," that is, not the texture constituted by the interwoven strands—then history, if it is set on dealing with the compound and not some meticulously selected ingredient of it, as it must be, will, in this sense, not be a science after all. A scientific cast of mind is seldom found together with historical curiosity or historical talent. We can make use of the techniques of the natural sciences to establish dates, order events in time and space, exclude untenable hypotheses and suggest new explanatory factors (as sociology, psychology, economics, medicine have so notably done), but the function of all these techniques, indispensable as they are to-day, can be no more than ancillary, for they are determined by their specific models, and are consequently "thin," whereas what the great historians sought to describe and analyse and explain is necessarily "thick": that is the essence of history, its purpose, its pride, and its reason for existence.

T. History, and other accounts of human life, are at times spoken of as being akin to art. What is usually meant is that writing about human life depends to a large extent on descriptive skill, style, lucidity, choice of examples, distribution of emphasis, vividness of characterization, and the like. But there is a profounder sense in which the historian's activity is an artistic one. Historical explanation is to a large degree arrangement of the discovered facts in patterns which satisfy us because they accord with life—the variety of human experience and activity—as we know it and can imagine it. That is the difference that distinguishes the humane studies—*Geisteswissenschaften*—from those of nature. When these patterns contain central concepts or categories that are ephemeral, or confined to trivial or unfamiliar aspects of human experience, we speak of such explanations as shallow, or inadequate, or eccentric, and find them unsatisfactory on those grounds. When these concepts are of wide scope, permanent, familiar, common to many men and many civilizations, we experience a sense of reality and dependability that derives from this very fact, and regard the explanation as well-founded, serious, satisfactory. On some occasions, seldom enough, the explanation not only involves, but reveals, basic categories of universal import, which, once they are forced upon consciousness, we recognise as underlying all our experience; yet so closely interwoven are they with all that we are and feel, and therefore so totally taken for granted, that to touch them at all is to communicate a shock to the entire system; the shock is one of recognition and one that may upset us, as is liable to happen when something deep-set and fundamental that has lain unquestioned and in darkness, is suddenly illuminated or prised out of its frame for closer inspection. When this occurs, and especially when the categories thus uncovered seem applicable to field after field of human activity, without apparent limits—so that we cannot tell how far they may yet extend—we call such explanations profound, fundamental, revolutionary, and those who proffer them—Vico, Kant, Marx, Freud—men of depth or insight and genius.

U. This kind of historical explanation is related to moral and aesthetic analysis, in so far as it presupposes conceiving of human beings not merely as organisms in space, the regularities of whose behaviour can be described and locked in labour saving formulae, but as active beings, pursuing ends, shaping their own and others' lives, feeling, reflecting, imagining, creating, in constant interaction and intercommunication with other human beings; in short, engaged in all the forms of experience that we understand because we share in them, and do not view them purely as external observers. This is what is called the inside view: and it renders possible and indeed inescapable explanation whose primary function is not to predict or extrapolate, or even control, but fit the loose and fleeting objects of sense, imagination, intellect, into the central succession of patterns that we call normal, and which is the ultimate criterion of reality as against illusion, incoherence, fiction. History is merely the mental projection into the past of this activity of selection and adjustment, the search for coherence and unity, together with the attempt to refine it with all the self-consciousness of which we are capable, by bringing to its aid everything that we conceive to be useful—all the sciences, all the knowledge and skills, and all the theories that we have acquired, from whatever quarter. This, indeed, is why we speak of the importance of allowing for imponderables in forming historical judgment, or of the faculty of judgment that seems mysterious only to those who start from the preconception that their induction, deduction and sense perception are the only legitimate sources of, or at least certified methods justifying claims to, knowledge. Those who, without mystical undertones, insist on the importance of common sense, or knowledge of life, or width of experience, or breadth of sympathy or imagination, or natural wisdom, or "depth" of insight—all normal and empirical attributes—are suspected of seeming to smuggle in some kind of illicit, metaphysical faculty only because the exercise of these gifts has relatively little value for those who deal with inanimate matter, for physicists or geologists. Capacity for understanding people's characters, knowledge of ways in which they are likely to react to one another, ability to "enter into" their motives, their principles, the movement of their thoughts and feelings (and this applies no less to the behaviour of masses or to the growth of cultures)—these are the talents that are indispensable to historians, but not (or not to such a degree) to natural scientists. The capacity for knowing that is like knowing someone's character or face, is as essential to historians as knowledge of facts. Without sufficient knowledge of facts an historical construction may be no more than a coherent fiction, a work of the romantic imagination; it goes without saying that if its claim to be true is to be sustained, it must be, as the generalizations which it incorporates must in their turn be, tethered to reality by verification of facts, as in any natural science. Nevertheless, even though in this ultimate sense what is meant by real and true is identical in science, in history and in ordinary life, yet the differences remain as great as the similarities.

V. This notion of what historians are doing when they are explaining may cast light also upon something that was mentioned earlier; namely, the idea of the inexorable succession of the stages of development, which made it not merely erroneous but absurd to suppose that *Hamlet* could have been written at the court of Genghis Khan, or that Richelieu could have pursued the policies realised by Bismarck. For this kind of certainty is not something that we derive from a careful inductive investigation of conditions in Outer Mongolia, as opposed to those of Elizabethan England, or the political relations between the great powers in the nineteenth century as opposed to those in the seventeenth, but from a more fundamental sense of what goes with what. We conceive of historical succession as being akin to that of the growth of the individual personality; to suggest that a child thinks or wills or acts like an old man, or *vice versa,* is something that we reject on the basis of our own direct experience (I mean by this not introspection, but knowledge of life—something that springs from interaction with others and with the surrounding environment and constitutes the sense of reality). Our conception of civilization is analogous to this. We do not feel it necessary to enumerate all the specific ways in which a wild nomad differs from a European of the Renaissance, or ask ourselves why it is—what inductive evidence we have for the contingent proposition that—the culture of the Renaissance is not merely different from, but represents a more mature phase of human growth than, that of Outer Mongolia two thousand years ago. The proposition that the culture of the Renaissance not merely did not precede, but cannot have preceded, the nomadic stage in the continuous development that we call a single culture, is something bound up so closely with our conception of how men live, of what societies are, of how they develop, indeed of the very meaning of the concepts of man, growth, society, that it is logically prior to our investigations and not their goal or product. It is not so much that it stands in no need of justification by their methods or results, as that it is logically absurd to bolster it up in this way. For this reason one might hesitate to call such knowledge empirical, for it is not confirmable or corrigible by the normal empirical methods, in relation to which it functions as base—as a frame of reference. But neither, of course, is it *a priori* (as Vico and Hegel, who showed original insight into this matter, sometimes imply) if by that is meant that it is obtainable in some special, non-naturalistic way. Recognition of the fundamental categories of human experience differs from both the acquisition of empirical information and deductive reasoning; such categories are logically prior to either, and are least subject to change among the elements that constitute our knowledge. Yet they are not alterable; and we can ask ourselves to what degree this or that change in them would affect our experience. It is possible, although *ex hypothesi* not easy, to conceive of beings whose fundamental categories of thought or perception radically differ from ours; the greater such differences, the harder it will be for us to communicate with them, or, if the process goes farther, to regard them as being human or sentient; or, if the process goes far enough, to conceive of them at all.

W. It is a corollary of this that one of the difficulties that beset historians and do not plague natural scientists, is that of reconstructing what occurred in the past not merely in terms of our own concepts and categories, but also of how such events must have looked to those who participated in or were affected by them—psychological facts that in their turn themselves influenced events. It is difficult enough to develop an adequate consciousness of what we are and what we are at, and how we have arrived where we have done, without also being called upon to make clear to ourselves what such consciousness and self-consciousness must have been like for persons in situations different from our own; yet no less is expected of the true historian. Chemists and physicists are not obliged to investigate the states of mind of Lavoisier or Boyle; still less of the unenlightened mass of men. Mathematicians need not worry themselves with the general outlook of Euclid or Newton. Economists *qua* economists need not grasp the inner vision of Adam Smith or Keynes, still less of their less gifted contemporaries. But it is the inescapable business of the historian who is more than a compiler or the slave of a doctrine or a party, to ask himself not merely what occurred (in the sense of publicly observable events), but also how the situation looked to various representative Greeks or Romans, or to Alexander or Julius Caesar, and above all to Thucydides, Tacitus or anonymous mediaeval chroniclers, or to Englishmen or Germans in the sixteenth century, or Frenchmen in 1789 or Russians in 1917, or to Luther, or Cromwell, or Robespierre or Lenin. This kind of imaginative projection of ourselves into the past, the attempt to capture concepts and categories that differ from those of the investigator by means of concepts and categories that cannot but be his own, is a task that he can never be sure that he is even beginning to achieve, yet is not permitted to abjure. He seeks to apply scientific tests to his conclusions, but this will take him but a little way. For it is a commonplace by now that the frontiers between fact and interpretation are blurred and shifting, and that what is fact from one perspective is interpretation from another. Even if chemical and palaeographic and archaeological methods yield some hard pebbles of indubitable fact, we cannot evade the task of interpretation, for nothing counts as an historical interpretation unless it attempts to answer the question of how the world must have looked to other individuals or societies if their acts and words are to be taken as the acts and words of human beings neither wholly like ourselves nor so different as not to fit into our common past. Without a capacity for sympathy and imagination beyond any required by a physicist, there is no vision of either past or present, neither of others nor of ourselves; but where it is wholly lacking, ordinary—as well as historical—thinking cannot function at all.

X. The contrast which I am trying to draw is not the difference between the two permanently opposed but complementary human demands: one for unity and homogeneity, the other for diversity and heterogeneity, which Kant has made so clear.[2] The contrast I mean is one between different types of knowledge. When the Jews are enjoined in the Bible to protect strangers "For ye know the soul of a stranger, seeing ye were strangers in the land of Egypt" (Exod. 23:9), this knowledge is neither deductive, nor inductive, nor founded on direct inspection, but akin to the "I know" of "I know what it is to be hungry and poor," or "I know how political bodies function," or "I know what it is to be a Brahmin." This is

2*Kritik der reinen Vernunft,* ed. Cassirer, III, p. 455.

neither (to use Professor Gilbert Ryle's useful classification) "knowing that" which the sciences provide, nor the "knowing how" which is the possession of a disposition or skill, nor the knowledge of direct perception, acquaintance, memory, but the type of knowledge that an administrator or politician must possess of the men with whom he deals. If the historian (or, for that matter, the contemporary commentator on events) is endowed with this too poorly, if he can fall back only on inductive techniques, then, however accurate his discoveries of fact, they remain those of an antiquarian, a chronicler, at best an archaeologist, but not those of an historian. It is not only erudition or belief in theories of human behaviour that enabled Marx or Namier to write history of the first order.

Perhaps some light may be cast on this issue by comparing historical method with that of linguistic or literary scholarship. No scholar could emend a text without a capacity (for which no technique exists) for "entering into the mind of" another society and age. Electronic brains cannot perform this: they can offer alternative combinations of letters but not choose between them successfully; since the infallible rules for "programming" have not been formulated. How do gifted scholars in fact arrive at their emendations? They do all that the most exacting natural science would demand; they steep themselves in the material of their authors; they compare, contrast, manipulate conbinations like the most accomplished cypher breakers, they may find it useful to apply statistical and quantitive methods, they formulate hypotheses and test them; all this may well be indispensable but it is not enough. In the end what guides them is a sense (which comes from study of the evidence) of what a given author could, and what he could not, have said; of what fits and what does not fit, into the general pattern of his thought. This, let me say again, is not the way in which we demonstrate that penicillin cures pneumonia.

Y. It might be that the deepest chasm which divides historical from scientific studies lies between the outlook of the external observer and of the actor. It is this that was brought out by the contrast between "inner" and "outer" which Vico initiated, and after him, the Germans, and is so suspect to modern positivists, between the questions "how?" or "what?" or "when?" on one side, and the questions "why?", "following what rule?", "towards what goal?", "springing from what motive?" on the other. It lies in the difference between the category of mere togetherness or succession (the correlations to which all sciences can in the end be reduced), and that of coherence and interpretation; between factual knowledge and understanding. The latter alone makes intelligible that celebrated identity in difference (which the Idealist philosophers exaggerated and abused) in virtue of which we conceive of one and the same outlook as being expressed in diverse manifestations, and perceive affinities (that are often difficult and at times impossible to formulate) between the dress of a society and its morals, its system of justice and the character of its poetry, its architecture and its domestic habits, its sciences and its religious symbols. This is Montesquieu's notorious "spirit" of the laws (or institutions) that belong to a society. Indeed, this alone gives its sense to the very notion of belonging;[3] without it we should not understand what is meant when something is described as belonging to, or as characteristic or typical of an age or a style or an outlook, nor, conversely, should we know what it is for some interpretation to be anachronistic, what is meant by an incompatibility between a given phenomenon and its alleged context in time; this type of misattribution is different in kind from formal inconsistency, a logical collision of theories or propositions. A concentrated interest in particular events or persons or situations as such,[4] and not as instances of a generalization, is a pre-requisite of that historical sense which, like sense of occasion

[3] Cf. p. 12 above.

[4] "There are really only two ways of acquiring knowledge of human affairs" says Ranke, "though the perception of the particular or through abstraction. . . . The former is the method of history. There is no other way. . . . Two qualities, I think, are required for the making of the true historian: first he must feel a participation and pleasure in the particular for itself. . . . Just as one takes delight in flowers without thinking to what genus of Linnaeus . . . they belong, without thinking how the whole manifests itself in the particular.

"Still this does not suffice; . . . while [the historian] reflects on the particular, the development of the world in general will become apparent to him." Quoted in *The Varieties of History*, pp. 58–59, ed. Fitz Stern (New York, 1956).

in agents intent on achieving some specific purpose, is sharpened by love or hate or danger; it is this that guides us in understanding, discovering and explaining. When historians assert particular propositions like "Lenin played a crucial role in making the Russian Revolution," or "Without Churchill England would have been defeated in 1940," the rational grounds for such assertions, whatever their degree of plausibility, are not identical with generalizations of the type "Such men, in such conditions, usually affect events in this fashion" for which the evidence may be exceedingly feeble; for we do not test the propositions solely—or indeed generally—by their logical links with such general propositions (or explanation sketches), but rather in terms of their coherence with our picture of a specific situation. To analyze this type of knowledge into a finite collection of general and particular, categorical and hypothetical, propositions, is not practicable. Every judgment that we formulate, whether in historical thought or ordinary life, involves general ideas and propositions without which there can be no thought or language. At times some among these generalizations can be clearly stated, and combined into models; where this occurs, natural sciences arise. But the descriptive and explanatory language of historians, because they seek to record or analyse or account for specific or even unique phenomena as such[5]—as often as not for their own sakes—cannot, for that reason, be reduced without residue to such general formulae, still less to models and their applications. Any attempt to do so will be halted at the outset by the discovery that the subject matter involves a "thick" texture of criss-crossing, constantly changing and melting conscious and unconscious beliefs and assumptions some of which it is impossible and all of which it is difficult to formulate, on which, nevertheless, our rational views and rational acts are founded, and, indeed, which they exhibit or articulate. This is the "web" of which Taine speaks, and it is possible to go only some way (it is impossible to say in advance how far) towards isolating and describing its ingredients if our rationality is challenged. And even if we succeed in making explicit all (which is absurd) or many (which is not practicable)

---

[5]All facts are, of course, unique, those dealt with by natural scientists no less than any others; but it is not their uniqueness that interests scientists.

or our general propositions or beliefs, this achievement will not take us much nearer the scientific ideal: for between a collection of generalizations—or unanalysed knots of them—and the construction of a model there still lies difficult or impassible country: the generalizations must exhibit an exceptional degree of constancy and logical connection, if this passage is to be negotiated.

What are we to call the faculty which an artist displays in choosing his material for his particular purpose; or which a politician or a publicist needs when he adopts a policy or presents a thesis, the success of which may depend on the degree of his sensitiveness to circumstances and to human characters, and to the specific interplay between them, with which, and upon which, he is working? The *Wirkungszusammenhang,* the general structure or pattern of experience—understanding of this may be uniquely valuable for scientists, but it is absolutely indispensable to the historian. Without it, he remains at best a chronicler or technical specialist; at worst a distorter and writer of inferior fiction. He may achieve accuracy, objectivity, lucidity, literary quality, breadth of knowledge, but unless he conveys a recognizable vision of life, and exhibits that sense of what fits into a given situation and what does not, which is the ultimate test of sanity, perception of a social *Gestalt,* not, as a rule, capable of being formalized in terms, let us say, of a field theory—unless he possesses a minimal capacity for this—the result is not recognised by us as an account of reality, that is, of what human beings, as we understand the term, could have felt or thought or done.

It was, I think, Professor Namier who once remarked about historical sense that there was no *a priori* short-cut to knowledge of the past; what actually happened can only be established by scrupulous empirical investigation, by research in its normal sense. What is meant by historical sense is the knowledge not of what happened, but of what did not happen. When an historian, in attempting to decide what occurred and why, rejects all the infinity of logically open possibilities, the vast majority of which are obviously absurd, and, like a detective, investigates only those possibilities which have at least some initial plausibility, it is this sense of what is plausible—what men, being men, could have done or been—that constitutes the sense of coherence with the patterns of life that I have tried to indicate. Such words as plausibility, likelihood, sense of reality, historical sense, are typical qualitative categories which distinguish historical studies as opposed to the natural sciences that seek to operate on a quantitative basis. This distinction, which originated in Vico and Herder, and was developed by Hegel and (*malgré soi*) Marx, Dilthey and Weber, is of fundamental importance.

Z. The gifts that historians need are different from those of the natural scientists. The latter must abstract, generalize, idealize, quantify, dissociate normally associated ideas (for nature is full of strange surprises, and as little as possible must be taken for granted), deduce, establish with certainty, reduce everything to the maximum degree of regularity, uniformity, and, so far as possible, to timeless repetitive patterns. Historians cannot ply their trade without a considerable capacity for thinking in general terms; but they need, in addition, peculiar attributes of their own: a capacity for integration, for perceiving qualitative similarities and differences, a sense of the unique fashion in which various factors combine in the particular concrete situation, which must at once be neither so unlike any other situation as to constitute a total break with the continuous flow of human experience, nor yet so stylized and uniform as to be the obvious creature of theory and not of flesh and blood. The capacities needed are rather those of association than of dissociation, of perceiving the relation of parts to wholes, of particular sounds or colours to the many possible tunes or pictures into which they might enter, of the links that connect individuals viewed and savoured as individuals, and not primarily as instances of types or laws. It is this that Hegel tried to put under the head of the synthesizing "Reason" as opposed to the analytic "Understanding"; and to provide it with a logic of its own. It is the "logic" that proved incapable of clear formulation or utility: it is this that cannot be incorporated in electronic brains. Such gifts relate as much to practice as to theory; perhaps to practice more directly. A man who lacks common intelligence can be a physicist of genius, but not even a mediocre historian. Some of the characteristics indispensable to (although not, by themselves, sufficient to move) historians are more akin to those needed in active human intercourse, than in the study or the laboratory or the cloister. The capacity for associating the fruits of experience in a manner that enables its possessors to distinguish, without the benefit of rules, what is central, permanent, or universal from what is local, or peripheral, or transient—that is what gives concreteness and plausibility, the breath of life, to historical accounts. Skill in establishing hypotheses by means of observation or memory or inductive procedures, while ultimately indispensable to the discovery of all forms of truth about the world, is not the rarest of the qualities required by historians, nor is the desire to find recurrences and laws itself a symptom of historical talent.

If we ask ourselves what historians have commanded the most lasting admiration, we shall, I think, find that they are neither the most ingenious, nor the most precise, nor even the discoverers of new facts or unsuspected causal connections, but those who (like imaginative writers) present men or societies or situations in many dimensions, at many intersecting levels simultaneously, writers in whose accounts human lives, and their relations both to each other and to the external world, are what (at our most lucid and imaginative) we know that they can be. The gifts the scientists most need are not these: they must be ready to call everything into question, to construct bold hypotheses unrelated to customary empirical procedures, and drive their logical implications as far as they will go, free from control by common sense or too great a fear of departing from what is normal or possible in the world. Only in this way will new truths and relations between them be found—truths which, in psychology or anthropology as well as physics or mathematics, do not depend upon preserving contact with common human experience. In this sense, to say of history that it should approximate to the condition of a science is to ask it to contradict its essence.

It would be generally agreed that the reverse of a grasp of reality is the tendency to fantasy or utopia. But perhaps there exist more ways than one to defy reality. May it not be that to be unscientific is to defy, for no good logical or empirical reason, established hypotheses and laws; while to be unhistorical is the opposite—to ignore or twist one's view of particular events, per-

sons, predicaments, in the name of laws, theories, principles derived from other fields, logical, ethical, metaphysical, scientific,
which the nature of the medium renders inapplicable? For what
else is it that is done by those theorists who are called fanatical
because their faith in a given pattern is not overcome by their
sense of reality? For this reason the attempt to construct a discipline which would stand to concrete history as pure to applied, no
matter how successful the human sciences may grow to be—even
if, as all but obscurantists must hope, they discover genuine,
empirically confirmed, laws of individual and collective behaviour—seems an attempt to square the circle. It is not a vain hope
for an ideal goal beyond human powers, but a chimera, born of
lack of understanding of the nature of natural science, or of
history, or of both.

3

THE MEANING OF HISTORY, I

If history is a way of understanding human experience, then it is not surprising that historians and others have looked to history to provide us with meaning to the human drama. One of the most persistent efforts in modern times to find meaning in history centers about the idea of progress. But we must say what we mean by progress in history. The idea developed in the seventeenth century, and by the end of the eighteenth century it was fully formed of four component parts: material progress, the progress of knowledge, progress of the mind, and social progress. But the nineteenth century added still another dimension to it, that of ideal progress, one that ran counter to the original intention.

The idea of progress was launched by Francis Bacon, Europe's earliest scientific spokesman to give us a full complement of the attitudes characteristic of the new discipline. Bacon was not the first to note that scientific knowledge is of a sort that accumulates, or is progressive, but he pointed out as well the reciprocal relation between knowing more and knowing how to do more. Modern man knew more than the ancients if only by virtue of the compass, gunpowder, and the printing press, certainly by virtue of the telescope, and these in turn assisted in the further development of science.

Thus the link was forged very early in the modern world between science and technology, with the expectation that technology could be made to contribute to the relief of man's estate and to the continuation of the progress man had made since antiquity. Progress of knowledge went hand in hand with material progress. Both were dependent, however, on a third kind of progress which determined all else: progress of the mind; for Bacon viewed science as an aspect of culture that has a civilizing mission.

What Bacon hoped for from the practice of science was, first, a willingness on the part of humans to be satisfied with less than absolute certainty—that is, an abandonment of the metaphysical quest for an unknowable absolute truth; second, the disinterested pursuit of truth that need not reflect personal prejudices; third, man's readiness to examine all the common assumptions of his age rather than be bound by the metaphors and formulas he himself creates; and fourth, the willingness to submit to no authority where it is a question of knowledge that each man may present by reasoning from evidence. By such mental attitudes, disciplined and made habitual, science would grow—for science is the only orthodoxy that thrives on self-correction—and growing, science would produce works useful to man. Finally, by redefining knowledge so as to limit it to science, and then defining science in terms of its method, Bacon hoped to enlarge the area of agreement among men, for no one quarrels forever about the descriptive laws of nature, only about what each group of men prescribes for itself. Thus Bacon ascribed to science the twin values of rationality and altruism, which were the mark of its early existence and the foundation for a belief in still another kind of progress, the progress of society.

The progress of society is promoted by science in stages of ever increasing refinement: from material progress to the progress of knowledge, to the progress of the mind through the increase of reason. The method of science became for the philosophers the heart of its structure since this method is self-regulating; that is, it provides the basis in reason for a critique of itself and for its own perpetual improvement. While the findings of science reduced men's ignorance, it was the method of science which freed their minds from credulity and from dependence on metaphysics, thereby contributing to an improved personal morality—one free of prejudice, dogmatism, and intolerance. By the very nature of his craft the successful scientist must avoid prejudging an issue, dogmatically asserting his conclusion, or being intolerant of divergent opinion. Social reformers in the eighteenth century found in these features of the scientific experience the qualities of a progressive society. In addition, they found the method of science applicable to other fields of thought.

If the growth of science has governed man's progress in the past, and science is defined in terms of its method, then the method of science is the principle of explanation in history. Also, if the progress of society is dependent in the future on the continuing growth of science, then discovery of the variables that condition its growth—freedom of thought, for example—provides us with the opportunity of furthering progress by increasing freedom. Thus according to the Enlightenment we have discovered one of the laws of social change. Armed with such knowledge, men can finally set about freeing their minds and bodies from the tyranny of church and state that characterized their past, and at last create a moral society. In this case what is needed to produce peace and well-being on earth is to educate man; he will then act to better his condition. Hence the liberal ideology of the Enlightenment was substantially moral. It borrowed from science the skeptical attitude of systematic doubt, and it discovered the uses of history. Given the undoubted fact of scientific progress, it is clear that we have made such progress in history, that is to say, in process. Progress is what distinguishes us from the past; process implies that we have continuity with the past, also with the future. Thus we can look to the future with hope for those good things, both mental and material, that will relieve man's age-old burdens. But the man who chooses progress must determine at any given moment what goals are progressive and what means are consistent with his purpose. He is forced to choose among alternatives, and in so doing the obligation to think clearly is a moral one. The Enlightenment argued for the pre-eminence of reason while speaking for the primacy of ethics, for only by the exercise of man's reason is the ethical life sustained. The identification of man's reason with his freedom was complete.

For the philosophers, science was a hopeful creed that had revolutionary implications. It is perhaps for this reason that social revolutionaries in the nineteenth century came to define history as a science. But the idea of a social science, as it developed in the nineteenth century, is unlike much that was known earlier as social progress. In the eighteenth century Nicolas Condorcet's support of science was concerned with the perfection of society only as it promotes each man's purpose: the increase of freedom and equality. For Condorcet history and science do not guarantee the betterment of man, but only provide him with the time and setting in which to be moral. Like other philosophers Condorcet thought that man controls his own destiny. He did not talk of necessary perfection, but of perfectability, or the capacity in man for earthly perfection. The philosophers perceived with ease that while science must serve an ethical purpose, ethics must not be modeled on scientific laws. To do so would be to misread science and ethics both, and thus to define **as** history what should be accomplished **in** history. For clearly the matter of science is descriptive; the matter of ethics is prescriptive. To establish progress as a necessary feature of history, as the nineteenth century did, might lend an air of scientific objectivity to our metaphysical musings, but it might also strip us of choice in the determination of our goals and actions. A science of society, however, either providential or positivistic, is precisely what the nineteenth century sought to devise, and in so doing it created a succession of "theodicies," which invested history with quasi-religious content. It is quite easy in fact easier, to do the same with science, to insist that what is in nature is what ought to be, but this as in history is to beg the epistemological question, how do we know?—and ultimately to foreclose on further investigation.

Perhaps the most significant effort in modern times to define meaning in history is G. W. F. Hegel's **Lectures in the Philosophy of History** (1836), which is at once a secular theodicy on the Augustinian model and a foundation of the view that history determines human consciousness. Thus Hegel solves the problem of moral meaning by declaring that history progresses toward moral betterment in conformity with God's plan for the world; but such betterment is accompanied, indeed achieved, by man's growing consciousness of the purpose and workings of history. Consequently, for Hegel meaning is immanent in history.

Hegel finds the source of reality in the Idea, or God, who is only implicit in nature but who expresses himself explicitly as Spirit in history. History is teleological, or purposive. The goal of history is Freedom, here defined as a moral condition of self-consciousness. History's instrument for achieving freedom is the Hero, the Alexanders and Napoleons who are used by "the cunning of Reason" to promote history's plan. The medium, both means and end, through which history speaks is the State, the epitome of social order at any given stage of history. Finally, the means for change in history is Reason, or the dialectic, a manifestation of Reason that functions in history to propel it toward its goal.

If we accept that thought and Idea are one, that the real is the rational, then it is possible to detail all of existence in a four-stage dialectic. The antithesis of Being is non-being, and the only synthesis that will encompass both, while raising being to a higher level, is consciousness. Idea's consciousness of its other is what makes possible a study of matter. The next higher stage that encompasses consciousness and non-consciousness is Reason, with which history begins. Finally, the course of history ends in Freedom, which is perfect consciousness of the truth. Man and Idea have become one. Being has had its beginning and end. Hence history is a theodicy; all is as it ought to be, or history has its Reason that man's reason knows not of. Freedom is one with necessity. It is actualized in the state and is expressed in law, which is the sum of morality. The state at any given moment is all these things: freedom, necessity, law, morality. To put it another way, the individual takes his historical reality from the state. His obedience to the state is the sum of his morality, for by such obedience he contributes to progress, which of course is foreordained by God. It is no wonder that in reaction to the Hegelian view of history so many historians turned subsequently to a "scientific" history, which did not, however, escape the suggestion that all is as it ought to be, except that it did not say so explicitly.

Tolstoy, as Isaiah Berlin describes him, was one of those who sought a grand design to history, and in a way more characteristic of the scientist than of the historian. Every scientist will look among the particulars for a generalization that will express them. Like Tolstoy he is a fox who wants to be a hedgehog; that is, he wants to see the forest for the trees. But even the scientist has given up looking for reality "as it really is," the thing-in-itself that we have no more way of knowing than we have of knowing God as He really is. Tolstoy, however, felt compelled to know not how power is used but what it really is, what words like "force" and "factor" in history really describe. He persisted in seeking an absolute that neither science nor history is capable of producing, no doubt because his own religious absolute failed him, forcing him to look for one elsewhere. And this in the face of his own lines about the battle of Borodino, where Pierre, echoing Voltaire's **Candide**, insists on an end to abstractions about war. In the end Tolstoy could arrive at no other absolute in history but death itself, when it is precisely life that the historian has to reckon with. The fact is that the problem in history of the hedgehog and the fox, the one versus the many, is a false one. The historian must, of course, be cognizant both of the one and the many, of unity and diversity, the particular and the universal, persistence and change, and himself create whatever meaning there is to be found in history.

In **What is History?** E. H. Carr argues very much the same way, but he unknowingly divides his work into two parts. There is little to debate with Carr when he tells us that history is an unending dialogue between the past and present, a movement between fact and interpretation, and that it is we who are obliged to create generalizations about history which alone contribute to our understanding of the past. But from talking about process he changes his meaning to progress. Carr defines progress as a coming to political consciousness of the masses, which he says has certainly worked to the good and will continue to do so in the future. He counsels us to ride the wave of the future. However, progress requires that we pay a price for it, which can only be paid in full consciousness of the cost. We may learn the cost from history, but it is we who elect to make progress; we cannot argue that history is the record of it except on faith. The future may always disappoint our expectations.

G. W. F. HEGEL

Reason in History

Reason is Thought determining itself in absolute freedom . . . .

It was for a while the fashion to admire God's wisdom in animals, plants, and individual lives. If it is conceded that Providence manifests itself in such objects and materials, why not also in world history? Because its scope seems to be too large. But the divine wisdom, or Reason, is the same in the large as in the small. We must not deem God to weak to exercise his wisdom on a grand scale. Our intellectual striving aims at recognizing that what eternal wisdom *intended* it has actually *accomplished,* dynamically active in the world, both in the realm of nature and that of the spirit. In this respect our method is a theodicy, a justification of God, which Leibniz attempted metaphysically, in his way, by undetermined abstract categories. Thus the evil in the world was to be comprehended and the thinking mind reconciled with it. Nowhere, actually, exists a larger challenge to such reconciliation than in world history. . . .

To begin with, we must note that world history goes on within the realm of Spirit . . . .

The nature of Spirit may be understood by a glance, at its direct opposite—Matter. The essence of matter is gravity, the essence of Spirit—its substance—is Freedom. It is immediately plausible to everyone that, among other properties, Spirit also possesses Freedom. But philosophy teaches us that *all* the properties of Spirit exist only through Freedom. All are but means of attaining Freedom; all seek and produce this and this alone. It is an insight of speculative philosophy that Freedom is the sole truth of Spirit. Matter possesses gravity by virtue of its tendency toward a central point; it is essentially composite, consisting of parts that exclude each other. It seeks its unity and thereby its own abolition; it seeks its opposite. If it would attain this it would be matter no longer, but would have perished. It strives toward ideality, for in unity it exists ideally. Spirit, on the contrary, is that which has its center in itself. It does not have unity outside of itself but has found it; it is in itself and with itself. Matter has its substance outside of itself; Spirit is Being-within-itself (self-contained existence). But this, precisely, is Freedom. For when I am dependent, I refer myself to something else which I am not; I cannot exist independently of something external. I am free when I am within myself. This self-contained existence of Spirit is self-consciousness, consciousness of self.

Two things must be distinguished in consciousness, first, *that* I know and, secondly, *what* I know. In self-consciousness the two coincide, for Spirit knows itself. It is the judgment of its own nature and, at the same time, the operation of coming to itself, to produce itself, to make itself (actually) into that which it is in itself (potentially). Following this abstract definition it may be said that world history is the exhibition of spirit striving to attain knowledge of its own nature. As the germ bears in itself the whole nature of the tree, the taste and shape of its fruit, so also the first traces of Spirit virtually contain the whole of history. Orientals do not yet know that Spirit—Man as such—is free. And because they do not know it, they are not free. They only know that *one* is free; but for this very reason such freedom is mere caprice, ferocity, dullness of passion, or, perhaps, softness and tameness of desire—which again is nothing but an accident of nature and thus, again, caprice. This *one* is therefore only a despot, not a free man. The consciousness of freedom first arose among the Greeks, and therefore they were free. But they, and the Romans likewise, only knew that some are free—not man as such. This not even Plato and Aristotle knew. For this reason the Greeks not only had slavery, upon which was based their whole life and the maintenance of their splendid liberty, but their freedom itself was partly an accidental, transient, and limited flowering and partly a severe thralldom of human nature. Only the Germanic peoples came, through Christianity, to realize that man as man is free and that freedom of Spirit is the very essence of man's nature. This realization first arose in religion, in the innermost region of spirit; but to introduce it in the secular world was a further task which could only be solved and fulfilled by a long and severe effort of civilization. Thus slavery did not cease immediately with the acceptance of the Christian religion. Liberty did not suddenly predominate in states nor reason in governments and constitutions. The application of the principle to secular conditions, the thorough molding and interpenetration of the secular world by it, is precisely the long process of history. I have already drawn attention to this distinction between a principle as such and its application, its introduction and execution in the actuality of life and spirit. This is a fundamental fact in our science and must be kept constantly in mind. Just as we noted it in the Christian principle of self-consciousness and freedom, so it shows itself in the principle of freedom in general. World history is the progress of the consciousness of freedom—a progress whose necessity we have to investigate . . . .

The insight then to which philosophy should lead us is that the actual world is as it ought to be, that the truly good, the universal divine Reason is the power capable of actualizing itself. This good, this Reason, in its most concrete representation, is God. God governs the world. The actual working of His government, the carrying out of His plan is the history of the world. Philosophy strives to comprehend this plan, for only that which has been carried out according to it has reality; whatever does not accord with it is but worthless existence . . . . What is the material in which the final end of Reason is to be realized? It is first of all the subjective agent itself, human desires, subjectivity in general. In human knowledge and volition, as its material basis, the rational attains existence. We have considered subjective volition with its purpose, namely, the truth of reality, insofar as moved by a great world-historical passion. As a subjective will in limited passions it is dependent; it can gratify its particular desires only within this dependence. But the subjective will has also a substantial life, a reality where it moves in the region of essential being and has the essential itself as the object of its existence. This essential being is the union of the subjective with the rational will; it is the moral whole, the *State*. It is that actuality in which the individual has and enjoys his freedom, but only as knowing, believing, and willing the universe. This must not be understood as if the subjective will of the individual attained its gratification and enjoyment through the common will and the latter were a means for it—as if the individual limited his freedom among the other individuals, so that this common limitation, the mutual constraint of all, might secure a small space of liberty for each. (This would only be negative freedom.) Rather, law, morality, the State, and they alone, are the positive reality and satisfaction of freedom. The caprice of the individual is not freedom. It is this caprice which is being limited, the license of particular desires.

The subjective will, passion, is the force which actualizes and realizes. The Idea is the interior; the State is the externally existing, genuinely moral life. It is the union of the universal and essential with the subjective will, and as such it is *Morality . . . .* The state is the divine Idea as it exists on earth.

Thus the State is the definite object of world history proper. In it freedom achieves its objectivity and lives in the enjoyment of this objectivity. For law is the objectivity of Spirit; it is will in its true form. Only the will that obeys the law is free, for it obeys itself and, being in itself, is free. In so far as the state, our country, constitutes a community of existence, and as the subjective will of man subjects itself to the laws, the antithesis of freedom and necessity disappears . . . .

History combines in our language the objective as well as the subjective side. It means both the *historiam rerum gestarum* and the *res gestas* themselves, both the events and the narration of the events. (It means both *Geschehen* and *Geschichte.*) This connection of the two meanings must be regarded as highly significant and not merely accidental. We must hold that the narration of history and historical deeds and events appear at the same time; a common inner principle brings them forth together . . . .

In work itself is implied the elemental character of universality, of Thought. Without Thought it has no objectivity; thought is its fundamental definition. The highest point of a people's development is the rational consciousness of its life and conditions, the scientific understanding of its laws, its system of justice, its morality. For in this unity (of subjective and objective) lies the most intimate unity in which Spirit can be with itself. The purpose of its work is to have itself as object. But Spirit can have itself as object only by thinking itself. . . .

Spirit is essentially the result of its own activity. Its activity is transcending the immediately given, negating it, and returning into itself. We can compare it with the seed of a plant, which is both beginning and result of the plant's whole life. The powerlessness of life manifests itself precisely in this falling apart of beginning and end. Likewise in the lives of individuals and peoples. The life of a people brings a fruit to maturity, for its activity aims at actualizing its principle. But the fruit does not fall back into the womb of the people which has produced and matured it. On the contrary, it turns into a bitter drink for this people. The people cannot abandon it, for it has an unquenchable thirst for it. But imbibing the drink is the drinker's destruction, yet, at the same time the rise of a new principle.

We have already seen what the final purpose of this process is. The principles of the national spirits progressing through a necessary succession of stages are only moments of the one universal Spirit which through them elevates and completes itself into a self-comprehending *totality*.

Thus, in dealing with the idea of Spirit only and in considering the whole of world history as nothing but its manifestation, we are dealing only with the *present*—however long the past may be which we survey. [*There is no time where it* (*the Spirit*) *has not been nor will not be; it neither was nor is it yet to be. It is forever* now.] The Idea is ever present, the Spirit immortal. [*What is true is eternal in and for itself, neither yesterday nor tomorrow but* now *in the sense of absolute presence. In the Idea, what may seem lost is eternally preserved.*] The implies that the present stage of Spirit contains all previous stages within itself. These, to be sure, have unfolded themselves successively and separately, but Spirit still is what it has in itself always been. The differentiation of its stages is but the development of what it is in itself. The life of the ever-present Spirit is a cycle of stages, which, on the one hand, co-exist side by side, but, on the other hand, seem to be past. The moments which Spirit seems to have left behind, it still possesses in the depth of its present.

ISAIAH BERLIN

The Hedgehog and the Fox

There is a line among the fragments of the Greek poet Archilochus which says: 'The fox knows many things, but the hedgehog knows one big thing." Scholars have differed about the correct interpretation of these dark words, which may mean no more than that the fox, for all his cunning, is defeated by the hedgehog's one defence. But, taken figuratively, the words can be made to yield a sense in which they mark one of the deepest differences which divide writers and thinkers, and, it may be, human beings in general. For there exists a great chasm between those, on one side, who relate everything to a single central vision, one system less or more coherent or articulate, in terms of which they understand, think and feel—a single, universal, organizing principle in terms of which alone all that they are and say has significance— and, on the other side, those who pursue many ends, often unrelated and even contradictory, connected, if at all, only in some *de facto* way, for some psychological or physiological cause, related by no moral or aesthetic principle; these last lead lives,

Sir Isaiah Berlin, *The Hedgehog and the Fox: An Essay on Tolstoy's View of History* (New York: New American Library, 1957), pp. 7–8, 11, 34–36, 44–45, 49–50, 58–59, 122, 123. Copyright 1953 by Simon & Schuster, Inc. Reprinted by permission of George Weidenfeld & Nicolson, Ltd., and Simon & Schuster, Inc.

perform acts, and entertain ideas that are centrifugal rather than centripetal, their thought is scattered or diffused, moving on many levels, seizing upon the essence of a vast variety of experiences and objects for what they are in themselves, without, consciously or unconsciously, seeking to fit them into, or exclude them from, any one unchanging, all-embracing, sometimes self-contradictory and incomplete, at times fanatical, unitary inner vision. The first kind of intellectual and artistic personality belongs to the hedge-hogs, the second to the foxes; and without insisting on a rigid classification, we may, without too much fear of contradiction, say that, in this sense, Dante belongs to the first category, Shake-speare to the second . . . . The hypothesis I wish to offer is that Tolstoy was by nature a fox, but believed in being a hedgehog; that his gifts and achievement are one thing, and his beliefs, and consequently his interpretation of his own achievement, another; and that consequently his ideals have led him, and those whom his genius for persuasion has taken in, into a systematic misinter-pretation of what he and others were doing or should be doing . . . . When Tolstoy contrasts this real life—the actual, ev-eryday, "live" experience of individuals—with the panoramic view conjured up by historians, it is clear to him which is real, and which is a coherent, some times elegantly contrived, but always fictitious construction. Utterly unlike her as he is in almost every other respect, Tolstoy is, perhaps, the first to propound the celebrated accusation which Virginia Woolf half a century later levelled against the public prophets of her own generation—Shaw and Wells and Arnold Bennett—blind materialists who did not begin to understand what it is that life truly consists of, who mistook its outer accidents, the unimportant aspects which lie outside the individual soul—the so-called social, economic, politi-cal realities—for that which alone is genuine, the individual ex-perience, the specific relation of individuals to one another, the colours, smells, tastes, sounds, and movements, the jealousies, loves, hatreds, passions, the rare flashes of insight, the transform-ing moments, the ordinary day-to-day succession of private data which constitute all there is—which are reality.

What, then, is the historian's task—to describe the ultimate data of subjective experience—the personal lives lived by men—

the "thoughts, knowledge, poetry, music, love, friendship, hates, passions" of which, for Tolstoy, "real" life is compounded, and only that? That was the task to which Turgenev was perpetually calling Tolstoy—him and all writers, but him in particular, because therein lay his true genius, his destiny as a great Russian writer; and this he rejected with violent indignation even during his middle years, before the final religious phase. For this was not to give the answer to the question of what there is, and why and how it comes to be and passes away, but to turn one's back upon it altogether, and stifle one's desire to discover how men live in society, and how they are affected by one another and by their environment, and to what end. This kind of artistic purism— preached in his day by Flaubert—this kind of preoccupation with the analysis and description of the experience and the relationships and problems and inner lives of individuals (later advocated and practised by Gide and the writers he influenced, both in France and in England) struck him as both trivial and false. He had no doubt about his own superlative skill in this very art—and that it was precisely this for which he was admired; and he condemned it absolutely. In a letter written while he was working on *War and Peace* he said with bitterness that he had no doubt that what the public would like best would be his scenes of social and personal life, his ladies and his gentlemen, with their petty intrigues, and entertaining conversations and marvellously described small idiosyncrasies.[1] But these are the trivial "flowers" of life, not the "roots." Tolstoy's purpose is the discovery of the truth, and therefore he must know what history consists of, and recreate only that. History is plainly not a science, and sociology, which pretends that it is, is a fraud; no genuine laws of history have been discovered, and the concepts in current use—"cause," "accident," "genius"—explain nothing: they are merely thin disguises for ignorance. Why do the events the totality of which we call history occur as they do? Some historians attribute events to the acts of individuals, but this is no answer: for they do not

---

[1] Cf. the profession of faith in his celebrated—and militantly moralistic—introduction to an edition of Maupassant whose genius, despite everything, he admires. He thinks much more poorly of Bernard Shaw whose social rhetoric he calls stale and platitudinous.

explain how these acts "cause" the events they are alleged to "cause" or "originate . . . ."

Tolstoy's central thesis—in some respects not unlike the theory of the inevitable "self-deception" of the *bourgeoisie* held by his contemporary Karl Marx, save that what Marx reserves for a class, Tolstoy sees in almost all mankind—is that there is a natural law whereby the lives of human beings no less than those of nature are determined; but that men, unable to face this inexorable process, seek to represent it as a succession of free choices, to fix responsibility for what occurs upon persons endowed by them with heroic virtues or heroic vices, and called by them "great men." What are great men? they are ordinary human beings, who are ignorant and vain enough to accept responsibility for the life of society, individuals who would rather take the blame for all the cruelties, injustices, disasters justified in their name, than recognize their own insignificance and impotence in the cosmic flow which pursues its course irrespective of their wills and ideals . . . . once man is involved in relationships with others, he is no longer free, he is part of the inexorable stream. Freedom is real, but it is confined to trivial acts. At other times even this feeble ray of hope is extinguished: Tolstoy declares that he cannot admit even small exceptions to the universal law; causal determinism is either wholly pervasive or it is nothing, and chaos reigns. Men's acts may seem free of the social nexus, but they are not free, they cannot be free, they are part of it. Science cannot destroy the consciousness of freedom, without which there is no morality and no art, but it can refute it. "Power" and "accident" are but names for ignorance of the causal chains, but the chains exist whether we feel them or not; fortunately we do not; for if we felt their weight, we could scarcely act at all; the loss of illusion would paralyse the life which is lived on the basis of our happy ignorance. But all is well: for we never shall discover all the causal chains that operate: the number of such causes is infinitely great, the causes themselves infinitely small; historians select an absurdly small portion of them and attribute everything to this arbitrarily chosen tiny section . . . .

[Tolstoy's] genius lay in the perception of specific properties, the almost inexpressible individual quality in virtue of which the given object is uniquely different from all others. Nevertheless he longed for a universal explanatory principle; that is the perception of resemblances or common origins, or single purpose, or unity in the apparent variety of the mutually exclusive bits and pieces which composed the furniture of the world.[2] Like all very penetrating, very imaginative, very clear-sighted analysts who dissect or pulverize in order to reach the indestructible core, and justify their own annihilating activities (from which they cannot abstain in any case) by the belief that such a core exists—he continued to kill his rivals' rickety constructions with cold contempt, as being unworthy of intelligent men, always hoping that the desperately-sought-for "real" unity would presently emerge from the destruction of the shams and frauds—the knock-kneed army of eighteenth- and nineteenth-century philosophies of history. And the more obsessive the suspicion that perhaps the quest was vain, that no core and no unifying principle would ever be discovered, the more ferocious the measures to drive this thought away by increasingly merciless and ingenious executions of more and more false claimants to the title of the truth. As Tolstoy moved away from literature to polemical writing this tendency became increasingly prominent: the irritated awareness at the back of his mind that no final solution was ever, in principle, to be found, caused Tolstoy to attack the bogus solutions all the more savagely for the false comfort they offered—and for being an insult to the intelligence.[3] . . . [Tolstoy] looked for a harmonious universe, but everywhere found war and disorder, which no attempt to cheat, however heavily disguised, could even begin to hide; and so, in a condition of final despair, he offered to throw away the terrible weapons of criticism, with which [he] was over-generously endowed, in favour of the single great vision, something too indivisi-

[2]Here the paradox appears once more; for the "infinitesimals", whose integration is the task of the ideal historian, must be reasonably uniform to make this operation possible; yet the sense of "reality" consists in the sense of their unique differences.

[3]In our day French existentialists for similar psychological reasons have struck out against all explanations as such because they are a mere drug to still serious questions, short-lived palliatives for wounds which are unbearable but must be borne, above all not denied or "explained"; for all explaining is explaining away, and that is a denial of the given—the existent—the brute facts.

bly simple and remote from normal intellectual processes to be assailable by the instruments of reason, and therefore, perhaps, offering a path to peace and salvation . . . . Tolstoy was the least superficial of men: he could not swim with the tide without being drawn irresistibly beneath the surface to investigate the darker depths below; and he could not avoid seeing what he saw and doubting even that; he could close his eyes but not forget that he was doing so; his appalling, destructive, sense of what was false frustrated this final effort at self-deception as it did all the earlier ones; and he died in agony, oppressed by the burden of his intellectual infallibility and his sense of perpetual moral error, the greatest of those who can neither reconcile, nor leave unreconciled, the conflict of what there is with what there ought to be.

E. H. CARR

What Is History?

The historian and the facts of history are necessary to one another. The historian without his facts is rootless and futile; the facts without their historian are dead and meaningless. My first answer therefore to the question, What is history?, is that it is a continuous process of interaction between the historian and his facts, an unending dialogue between the present and the past . . . . The reciprocal process of interaction between the historian and his facts, what I have called the dialogue between present and past, is a dialogue not between abstract and isolated individuals, but between the society of today and the society of yesterday. History, in Burckhardt's words, is "the record of what one age finds worthy of note in another."[1] The past is intelligible to us only in the light of the present; and we can fully understand the present only in the light of the past. To enable man to understand the society of the past and to increase his mastery over the society of the present is the dual function of history . . . .

[1]Burckhardt: *Judgments on History and Historians,* p. 158.

History is a process of struggle in which results, whether we judge them good or bad, are achieved by some groups directly or indirectly—and more often directly than indirectly—at the expense of others. The losers pay. Suffering is indigenous in history. Every great period of history has its casualties as well as its victories. This is an exceedingly complicated question because we have no measure which enables us to balance the greater good of some against the sacrifices of others: yet some such balance must be struck. It is not exclusively a problem of history. In ordinary life we are more often involved than we sometimes care to admit in the necessity of preferring the lesser evil, or of doing evil that good may come. In history the question is sometimes discussed under the rubric "the cost of progress" or "the price of revolution." This is misleading. As Bacon says in the essay *On Inovations,* "the forward retention of custom is as turbulent a thing as an innovation." The cost of conservation falls just as heavily on the under-privileged as the cost of innovation on those who are deprived of their privileges. The thesis that the good of some justifies the sufferings of others is implicit in all government, and is just as much a conservative as a radical doctrine. Dr. Johnson robustly invoked the argument of the lesser evil to justify the maintenance of existing inequalities:

> It is better that some should be unhappy than that none should be happy, which would be the case in a general state of equality.[2] . . .

But does not the fact that the historian, unlike the scientist, becomes involved by the nature of his material in these issues of moral judgment imply the submission of history to a super-historical standard of value? I do not think that it does. Let us assume that abstract conceptions like "good" and "bad," and more sophisticated developments of them, lie beyond the confines of history. But, even so, these abstractions play in the study of historical morality much the same role as mathematical and logi-

[2]Boswell: *Life of Doctor Johnson,* 1776 (Everyman ed. ii, 20). This has the merit of candour; Burckhardt (*Judgments on History and Historians,* p. 85) sheds tears over the "silenced moans" of the victims of progress, "who, as a rule, had wanted nothing else but *parta tueri,*" but is himself silent about the moans of the victims of the *ancien régime* who, as a rule, had nothing to preserve.

cal formulas in physical science. They are indispensable categories of thought; but they are devoid of meaning or application till
specific content is put into them. If you prefer a different meta-
phor, the moral precepts which we apply in history or in everyday
life are like cheques on a bank: they have a printed and a written
part. The printed part consists of abstract words like liberty and
equality, justice and democracy. These are essential categories.
But the cheque is valueless until we fill in the other part, which
states how much liberty we propose to allocate to whom, whom
we recognize as our equals, and up to what amount. The way in
which we fill in the cheque from time to time is a matter of
history. The process by which specific historical content is given to
abstract moral conceptions is a historical process; indeed, our
moral judgments are made within a conceptual framework which
is itself the creation of history. The favourite form of contemporary international controversy on moral issues is a debate on
rival claims to freedom and democracy. The conceptions are
abstract and universal. But the content put into them has varied
throughout history, from time to time and from place to place;
any practical issue of their application can be understood and
debated only in historical terms . . . . History is movement; and
movement implies comparison. That is why historians tend to
express their moral judgments in words of a comparative nature like
"progressive" and "reactionary" rather than in uncompromising
absolutes like "good" and "bad"; these are attempts to define
different societies or historical phenomena not in relation to some
absolute standard, but in their relation to one another. Moreover,
when we examine these supposedly absolute and extra-historical
values, we find that they too are in fact rooted to history. The
emergence of a particular value or ideal at a given time or place
is explained by historical conditions of place and time. The practical content of hypothetical absolutes like equality, liberty, justice,
or natural law varies from period to period, or from continent to
continent. Every group has its own values which are rooted in
history. Every group protects itself against the intrusion of alien
and inconvenient values, which it brands by opprobrious epithets
as bourgeois and capitalist, or undemocratic and totalitarian, or,

more crudely still, as un-English and un-American. The abstract standard or value, divorced from society and divorced from history, is as much an illusion as the abstract individual. The serious historian is the one who recognizes the historically conditioned character of all values, not the one who claims for his own values an objectivity beyond history. The beliefs which we hold and the standards of judgment which we set up are part of history, and are as much subject to historical investigation as any other aspect of human behaviour. Few sciences today—least of all, the social sciences—would lay claim to total independence. But history has no fundamental dependence on something outside itself which would differentiate it from any other science. . . . Scientists, social scientists, and historians are all engaged in different branches of the same study: the study of man and his environment, of the effects of man on his environment and of his environment on man. The object of the study is the same: to increase man's understanding of, and mastery over, his environment. The presuppositions and the methods of the physicist, the geologist, the psychologist, and the historian differ widely in detail; nor do I wish to commit myself to the proposition that, in order to be more scientific, the historian must follow more closely the methods of physical science. But historian and physical scientist are united in the fundamental purpose of seeking to explain, and in the fundamental procedure of question and answer. The historian, like any other scientist, is an animal who incessantly asks the question: Why? . . . The world of the historian, like the world of the scientist, is not a photographic copy of the real world, but rather a working model which enables him more or less effectively to understand it and to master it. The historian distils from the experience of the past, or from so much of the experience of the past as is accessible to him, that part which he recognizes as amenable to rational explanation and interpretation, and from it draws conclusions which may serve as a guide to action. A recent popular writer, speaking of the achievements of science, refers graphically to the processes of the human mind which, "rummaging in the ragbag of observed 'facts,' selects, pieces, and patterns the *relevant* observed facts together, rejecting the *irrelevant,* until

it has sewn together a logical and rational quilt of 'knowledge,' "[3] With some qualification as to the dangers of undue
subjectivism, I should accept that as a picture of the way in which
the mind of the historian works. . . .

At this juncture, it is time for me to confess to a rather shabby
trick which I have played on you, though, since you will have had
no difficulty in seeing through it, and since it has enabled me on
several occasions to shorten and simplify what I had to say, you
will perhaps have been indulgent enough to treat it as a convenient piece of shorthand. I have hitherto consistently used the
conventional phrase "past and present." But, we all know, the
present has no more than a notional existence as an imaginary
dividing line between the past and the future. In speaking of the
present, I have already smuggled another time dimension into the
argument. It would, I think, be easy to show that, since past and
future are part of the same time-span, interest in the past and
interest in the future are interconnected. The line of demarcation
between pre-historic and historical times is crossed when people
cease to live only in the present, and become consciously interested both in their past and their future. History begins with the
handing down of tradition; and tradition means the carrying of
the habits and lessons of the past into the future. Records of the
past begin to be kept for the benefit of future generations. "Historical thinking," writes the Dutch historian Huizinga, "is always
teleological."[4] Sir Charles Snow recently wrote of Rutherford that
"like all scientists . . . he had, almost without thinking what it
meant, the future in his bones."[5] Good historians, I suspect,
whether they think about it or not, have the future in their bones.
Besides the question: Why? the historian also asks the question:
Whither? . . .

The other day I was shocked to come across, I think,
the only remark of Bertrand Russell I have ever seen which
seemed to me to betray an acute sense of class: "There is,

---

[3]Leslie Paul: *The Annihilation of Man* (London: Faber & Faber; 1944), p. 147.

[4]J. Huizinga translated in *Varieties of History*, ed. F. Stern (London: Thames &
Hudson; 1957), p. 293.

[5]*The Baldwin Age*, ed. John Raymond (London: Eyre & Spottiswoode; 1960),
p. 246.

on the whole, much less liberty in the world now than there was a hundred years ago."[6] I have no measuring-rod for liberty, and do not know how to balance the lesser liberty of few against the greater liberty of many. But on any standard of measurement I can only regard the statement as fantastically untrue. I am more attracted by one of those fascinating glimpses which Mr. A. J. P. Taylor sometimes gives us into Oxford academic life. All this talk about the decline of civilization, he writes, "means only that university professors used to have domestic servants and now do their own washing-up."[7] Of course, for former domestic servants, washing-up by professors may be a symbol of progress. The loss of white supremacy in Africa, which worries Empire loyalists, Africaner republicans and investors in gold and copper shares, may look like progress to others. I see no reason why, on this question of progress, I should *ipso facto* prefer the verdict of the 1950's to that of the 1890's, the verdict of the English-speaking world to that of Russia, Asia, and Africa, or the verdict of the middle-class intellectual to that of the man in the street who, according to Mr. Macmillan, has never had it so good. . . .

We need not trouble ourselves with the question when progress— or civilization—began. The hypothesis of a finite end of progress has led to more serious misapprehension. Hegel has been rightly condemned for seeing the end of progress in the Prussian monarchy—apparently the result of an overstrained interpretation of his view of the impossibility of prediction. But Hegel's aberration was capped by that eminent Victorian, Arnold of Rugby, who in his inaugural lecture as Regius Professor of Modern History in Oxford in 1841 thought that modern history would be the last stage in the history of mankind: "It appears to bear marks of the fullness of time, as if there would be no future history beyond it."[8] Marx's prediction that the proletarian revolution would realize the ultimate aim of a classless society was logically and morally less vulnerable; but the presumption of an end of history has an eschatological ring more appropriate to the theologian than

[6]Russell: *Portraits From Memory*, p. 124.

[7]*The Observer* (June 21, 1959).

[8]T. Arnold: *An Inaugural Lecture on the Study of Modern History* (1841), p. 38.

to the historian, and reverts to the fallacy of a goal outside history. No doubt a finite end has attractions for the human mind; and Acton's vision of the march of history as an unending progress towards liberty seems chilly and vague. But if the historian is to save his hypothesis of progress, I think he must be prepared to treat it as a process into which the demands and conditions of successive periods will put their own specific content. And this is what is meant by Acton's thesis that history is not only a record of progress, but a "progressive science," or, if you like, that history in both senses of the word—as the course of events and as the record of those events—is progressive. . . . For the historian the end of progress is not already evolved. It is something still infinitely remote; and pointers towards it come in sight only as we advance. This does not diminish its importance. A compass is a valuable and indeed indispensable guide. But it is not a chart of the route. The content of history can be realized only as we experience it . . . .

No sane person ever believed in a kind of progress which advanced in an unbroken straight line without reverses and deviations and breaks in continuity so that even the sharpest reverse is not necessarily fatal to the belief. Clearly there are periods of regression as well as periods of progress. . . . the effort which is needed to drive civilization forward dies away in one place and is later resumed at another, so that whatever progress we can observe in history is certainly not continuous either in time or in place. Indeed, if I were addicted to formulating laws of history, one such law would be to the effect that the group—call it a class, a nation, a continent, a civilization, what you will—which plays the leading role in the advance of civilization in one period is unlikely to play a similar role in the next period, and this for the good reason that it will be too deeply imbued with the traditions, interests, and ideologies of the earlier period to be able to adapt itself to the demands and conditions of the next period.[9] Thus it

[9]For a diagnosis of such a situation, see R. S. Lynd: *Knowledge for What?* (Princeton University Press; 1939), p. 88: "Elderly people in our culture are frequently oriented towards the past, the time of their vigour and power, and resist the future as a threat. It is probable that a whole culture in an advanced stage of loss of relative power and disintegration may thus have a dominant orientation towards a lost golden age, while life is lived sluggishly along in the present."

may very well happen that what seems for one group a period of decline may seem to another the birth of a new advance. Progress does not and cannot mean equal and simultaneous progress for all. It is significant that almost all our latter-day prophets of decline, our sceptics who see no meaning in history and assume that progress is dead, belong to that sector of the world and to that class of society which have triumphantly played a leading and predominant part in the advance of civilization for several generations. It is no consolation to them to be told that the role which their group has played in the past will now pass to others. Clearly a history which has played so scurvy a trick on them cannot be a meaningful or rational process. But, if we are to retain the hypothesis of progress, we must, I think, accept the condition of the broken line . . . .

It is presupposition of history that man is capable of profiting (not that he necessarily profits) by the experience of his predecessors, and that progress in history, unlike evolution in nature, rests on the transmission of acquired assets. These assets include both material possessions and the capacity to master, transform, and utilize one's environment. Indeed, the two factors are closely interconnected, and react on one another . . . . The notion of a finite and clearly definable goal of progress in history, so often postulated by nineteenth-century thinkers, has proved inapplicable and barren. Belief in progress means belief not in any automatic or inevitable process, but in the progressive development of human potentialities. Progress is an abstract term; and the concrete ends pursued by mankind arise from time to time out of the course of history, not from some source outside it. I profess no belief in the perfectibility of man, or in a future paradise on earth. To this extent I would agree with the theologians and the mystics who assert that perfection is not realizable in history. But I shall be content with the possibility of unlimited progress—or progress subject to no limits that we can need or envisage— towards goals which can be defined only as we advance towards them, and the validity of which can be verified only in a process of attaining them. Nor do I know how, without some such conception of progress, society can survive. Every civilized society imposes sacrifices on the living generation for the sake of generations yet unborn. To justify these sacrifices in the name of a better world in the future is the secular counterpart of justifying them in the name of some divine purpose. In Bury's words, "the principle of duty to posterity is a direct corollary of the idea of progress."[10] Perhaps this duty does not require justification. If it does, I know of no other way to justify it.

This brings me to the famous crux of objectivity in history. The word itself is misleading and question-begging. In an earlier lecture I have already argued that the social sciences—and history among them—cannot accommodate themselves to a theory of knowledge which puts subject and object asunder, and enforces a rigid separation between the observer and the thing observed. We need a new model which does justice to the complex process of interrelation and interaction between them. The facts of history cannot be purely objective, since they become facts of history only in virtue of the significance attached to them by the historian. Objectivity in history—if we are still to use the conventional term—cannot be an objectivity of fact, but only of relation, of the relation between fact and interpretation, between past, present, and future. I need not revert to the reasons which led me to reject as unhistorical the attempt to judge historical events by erecting an absolute standard of value outside history and independent of it. But the concept of absolute truth is also not appropriate to the world of history—or, I suspect, to the world of science. It is only the simplest kind of historical statement that can be adjudged absolutely true or absolutely false. At a more sophisticated level, the historian who contests, say, the verdict of one of his predecessors will normally condemn it, not as absolutely false, but as inadequate or one-sided or misleading, or the product of a point of view which has been rendered obsolete or irrelevant by later evidence. To say that the Russian revolution was due to the stupidity of Nicholas II or to the genius of Lenin is altogether inadequate—so inadequate as to be altogether misleading. But it cannot be called absolutely false. The historian does not deal in absolutes of this kind. . . .

The absolute in history is not something in the past from which we start; it is not something in the present, since all present

[10]Bury: *The Idea of Progress*, p. ix.

thinking is necessarily relative. It is something still incomplete and in process of becoming—something in the future towards which we move, which begins to take shape only as we move towards it, and in the light of which, as we move forward, we gradually shape our interpretation of the past. This is the secular truth behind the religious myth that the meaning of history will be revealed in the day of judgment. Our criterion is not an absolute in the static sense of something that is the same yesterday, today, and forever: such an absolute is incompatible with the nature of history. But it is an absolute in respect of our interpretation of the past. It rejects the relativist view that one interpretation is as good as another, or that every interpretation is true in its own time and place, and it provides the touchstone by which our interpretation of the past will ultimately be judged. It is this sense of direction in history which alone enables us to order and interpret the events of the past—the task of the historian—and to liberate and organize human energies in the present with a view to the future—the task of the statesman, the economist, and the social reformer. But the process itself remains progressive and dynamic. Our sense of direction, and our interpretation of the past, are subject to constant modification and evolution as we proceed. . . . It is at once the justification and the explanation of history that the past throws light on the future, and the future throws light on the past.

What, then, do we mean when we praise a historian for being objective, or say that one historian is more objective than another? Not, is is clear, simply that he gets his facts right, but rather that he chooses the right facts, or, in other words, that he applies the right standard of significance. When we call a historian objective, we mean, I think, two things. First of all, we mean that he has a capacity to rise above the limited vision of his own situation in society and in history—a capacity which, as I suggested in an earlier lecture, is partly dependent on his capacity to recognize the extent of his involvement in that situation, to recognize, that is to say, the impossibility of total objectivity. Secondly, we mean that he has the capacity to project his vision into the future in such a way as to give him a more profound and more lasting insight into the past than can be attained by those historians whose outlook is entirely bounded by their own immediate situation. No historian today will echo Acton's confidence in the prospect of "ultimate history." But some historians write history which is more durable, and has more of this ultimate and objective character, than others; and these are the historians who have what I may call a long-term vision over the past and over the future. The historian of the past can make an approach towards objectivity only as he approaches towards the understanding of the future.

When, therefore, I spoke of history in an earlier lecture as a dialogue between past and present, I should rather have called it a dialogue between the events of the past and progressively emerging future ends. The historian's interpretation of the past, his selection of the significant and the relevant, evolves with the progressive emergence of new goals. To take the simplest of all illustrations, so long as the main goal appeared to be the organization of constitutional liberties and political rights, the historian interpreted the past in constitutional and political terms. When economic and social ends began to replace constitutional and political ends, historians turned to economic and social interpretations of the past. In this process, the sceptic might plausibly allege that the new interpretation is no truer than the old; each is true for its period. Nevertheless, since the preoccupation with economic and social ends represents a broader and more advanced stage in human development than the preoccupation with political and constitutional ends, so the economic and social interpretation of history may be said to represent a more advanced stage in history than the exclusively political interpretation. The old interpretation is not rejected, but is both included and superseded in the new. Historiography is a progressive science in the sense that it seeks to provide constantly expanding and deepening insights into a course of events which is itself progressive. This is what I should mean by saying that we need "a constructive outlook over the past." Modern historiography has grown up during the past two centuries in this dual belief in progress, and cannot survive without it, since it is this belief which provided it with its standard of significance, its touchstone for distinguishing between the real and the accidental. Goethe, in a conversation towards the end of his life, cut the Gordian knot a little brusquely:

When eras are on the decline, all tendencies are subjective; but on the other hand when matters are ripening for a new epoch, all tendencies are objective.[11]

Nobody is obliged to believe either in the future of history or in the future of society. It is possible that our society may be destroyed or may perish of slow decay, and that history may relapse into theology—that is to say, a study not of human achievement, but of the divine purpose—or into literature—that is to say, a telling of stories and legends without purpose or significance. But this will not be history in the sense in which we have known it in the last two hundred years . . . . The historian, as I said in my first lecture, is balanced between fact and interpretation, between fact and value. He cannot separate them. It may be that, in a static world, you are obliged to pronounce a divorce between fact and value. But history is meaningless in a static world. History in its essence is change, movement or—if you do not cavil at the old-fashioned word—progress.

I return therefore in conclusion to Acton's description of progress as "the scientific hypothesis on which history is to be written." You can, if you please, turn history into theology by making the meaning of the past depend on some extra-historical and superrational power. You can, if you please, turn it into literature—a collection of stories and legends about the past without meaning or significance. History properly so-called can be written only by those who find and accept a sense of direction in history itself. The belief that we have come from somewhere is closely linked with the belief that we are going somewhere. A society which has lost belief in its capacity to progress in the future will quickly cease to concern itself with its progress in the past. As I said at the beginning of my first lecture, our view of history reflects our view of society. I now come back to my starting-point by declaring my faith in the future of society and in the future of history . . . .

History begins when men begin to think of the passage of time in terms not of natural processes—the cycle of the seasons, the

---

[11]Quoted in J. Huizinga: *Men and Ideas* (New York: Meridian Books; 1959), p. 50.

human life-span—but of a series of specific events in which men are consciously involved and which they can consciously influence. History, says Burckhardt, is "the break with nature caused by the awakening of consciousness."[12] History is the long struggle of man, by the exercise of his reason, to understand his environment and to act upon it. But the modern period has broadened the struggle in a revolutionary way. Man now seeks to understand, and to act on, not only his environment, but himself; and this has added, so to speak, a new dimension to reason, and a new dimension to history. The present age is the most historically minded of all ages. Modern man is to an unprecedented degree self-conscious and therefore conscious of history. He peers eagerly back into the twilight out of which he has come in the hope that its faint beams will illuminate the obscurity into which he is going; and, conversely, his aspirations and anxieties about the path that lies ahead quicken his insight into what lies behind. Past, present, and future are linked together in the endless chain of history . . . .

Modern history begins when more and more people emerge into social and political consciousness, become aware of their respective groups as historical entities having a past and a future, and enter fully into history. It is only within the last two hundred years at most, even in a few advanced countries, that social, political, and historical consciousness has begun to spread to anything like a majority of the population. It is only today that it has become possible for the first time even to imagine a whole world consisting of peoples who have in the fullest sense entered into history and become the concern, no longer of the colonial administrator or of the anthropologist, but of the historian. This is a revolution in our conception of history . . . . Progress in human affairs, whether in science or in history or in society, has come mainly through the bold readiness of human beings not to confine themselves to seeking piecemeal improvements in the way things are done, but to present fundamental challenges in the name of reason to the current way of doing things and to the avowed or hidden assumptions on which it rests. I look forward to

[12]Burckhardt: *Reflections on History* (London: George Allen & Unwin; 1959), p. 31.

a time when the historians and sociologists and political thinkers of the English-speaking world will regain their courage for that task.

It is, however, not the waning of faith in reason among the intellectuals and the political thinkers of the English-speaking world which perturbs me most, but the loss of the pervading sense of a world in perpetual motion. This seems at first sight paradoxical; for rarely has so much superficial talk been heard of changes going on around us. But the significant thing is that change is no longer thought of as achievement, as opportunity, as progress, but as an object of fear. When our political and economic pundits prescribe, they have nothing to offer us but the warning to mistrust radical and far-reaching ideas, to shun anything that savours of revolution, and to advance—if advance we must—as slowly and cautiously as we can. At a moment when the world is changing its shape more rapidly and more radically than at any time in the last four hundred years, this seems to me a singular blindness, which gives ground for apprehension, not that the world-wide movement will be stayed, but that this country—and perhaps other English-speaking countries—may lag behind the general advance, and relapse helplessly and uncomplainingly into some nostalgic backwater. For myself I remain an optimist; and when Sir Lewis Namier warns me to eschew programmes and ideals, and Professor Oakeshott tells me that we are going nowhere in particular and that all that matters is to see that nobody rocks the boat, and Professor Popper wants to keep that dear old T-model on the road by dint of a little piecemeal engineering, and Professor Trevor-Roper knocks screaming radicals on the nose, and Professor Morison pleads for history written in a sane conservative spirit, I shall look out on a world in tumult and a world in travail, and shall answer in the well-worn words of a great scientist: "And yet—it moves."

4

THE MEANING OF HISTORY, II

Modern efforts from Hegel to Carr to find redemption in history have met with objection from theologians like Reinhold Niebuhr who argue rightly that history can guarantee no such thing. This should be easy to understand once it is recognized that the business of history is with the past and not with the future. Hence, "there is no possibility of a final judgment within history but only at the end of history . . . . History, in short, does not solve the enigma of history." Only a transhistorical explanation of life will do that, and traditional religion has already made one available to us. Its virtue for the believer is that it provides him with a theodicy that allows effort toward human betterment but does not require him to believe, in the face of the evidence, that such betterment is automatically achieved.

The sense of history grew out of an idea of progress, as we have noted earlier. But the proposition is not reversible. Progress is not guaranteed by history. To insist that it is, is to secularize the providential idea of history. With this view of history God's ways are inscrutable to man, so that man has unfortunately no other destiny than what happens to him. Few contemporary theologians would subscribe to that view. A valid idea of progress, on the contrary, is a humanistic one requiring us to work in behalf of progress that we ourselves define, with no assurance of course that we are correct in our definition or in any of our measures, and with no certainty that we shall agree on the matter. Still we must act on behalf of one proposition or another, and normally we do so on some ethical ground. Only the human individual is a moral agent, never history as such, or the working class, or the German **Volk**, or what have you. (Truth in history is the result not of laws that history obeys, but of our obedience to the rules of evidence.) We can know progress only by the specific goals we choose and the distance we travel to reach them. We cannot say that things as they are will somehow conduce to the good of mankind; we would have to say, if we are being honest, that we prefer leaving them as they are because the price for doing otherwise might be more than we are willing to pay. Once we acknowledge this to ourselves, all attempts at a secular theodicy, even the tacit ones, fall to the ground.

Arnold Toynbee is guilty of no such theodicy. On the contrary, he finds on historical evidence that unless we mend our ways our civilization is doomed to be extinguished, as so many others were. But according to what principle should we behave in order to save ourselves? It is here that Toynbee's explanation of history, hedgehog in character, becomes evident, for he would have us recognize that history is guided primarily by our spiritual needs quite as much as Marx would have us believe it is guided by our material ones. We recognize, as well, that for all Toynbee's show of scientific apparatus and empirical expertise he is guided in his researches by an a priori commitment to religious values. Such a commitment allows Toynbee to believe that in the world's encounter with the West, "the scroll of history has already been unrolled from beginning to end . . . [that] our future can perhaps be deciphered in this record of a Graeco-Roman past." That belief has given rise to Pieter Geyl's charge that "the Student of History, as Toynbee calls himself . . . may know more of history than I shall ever do, but he is no historian. He is a prophet." The study of the past does not allow us to predict the future. At best it can allow us only to anticipate it.

Pieter Geyl's purpose in the selection included here is to debate Toynbee's thesis, but in the process he has things to say that clarify our understanding of history. History, he argues, yields no more certitude than science does. Indeed, it is a misunderstanding on Toynbee's part to believe that science does yield certitude, and may explain his trust in a scientific apparatus. Even so, Toynbee's system "is essentially . . . irrational and a prioristic," as we have indicated. "By presenting it under the guise of scientific method and empiricism he not only revolts the scholar in me but he rouses me to protest, because I believe that clear thinking is perhaps the most crying need of our distracted world." Clear thinking compels us to admit that the "multitudinous movement of history" offers no consoling meaning, that the historian may not approach the past with a single principle or dogma of overwhelming magnitude. History remains for Geyl not a dialectical process with a certain end, but a never-ending dialogue between past and present in which the present may ultimately learn more about itself than it does about the past, and in which the lessons of history may never be applied with confidence to the future.

REINHOLD NIEBUHR

Faith and History

The history of mankind exhibits no more ironic experience than the contrast between the sanguine hopes of recent centuries and the bitter experiences of contemporary man. Every technical advance, which previous generations regarded as a harbinger or guarantor of the redemption of mankind from its various difficulties, has proved to be the cause, or at least the occasion, for a new dimension of ancient perplexities.

A single article of faith has given diverse forms of modern culture the unity of a shared belief. Modern men of all shades of opinion agreed in the belief that historical development is a redemptive process. It was the genuine achievement of modern historical science to discover that human culture is subject to indeterminate development. Natural science added the discovery that nature, as well as human culture and institutions, undergoes an evolutionary process. Thus the static conception of history which characterized the Middle Ages as well as antiquity was breached. It would be more accurate to say that the discoveries of the historical and natural sciences gave modern men a final justification for a new faith which had been developing since the

Renaissance. Joachim of Flores had given the first intimation of it in the late Middle Ages when he transmuted Christian eschatology into the hope of a transfigured world, of a future age of the Holy Spirit, in which the antinomies and ambiguities of man's historic existence would be overcome in history itself.

The Renaissance, which ostensibly restored classical learning, was actually informed by a very unclassical sense of history. It retained, or returned to, the cyclical interpretation of history, as known in the classical age; but historical cycles became spirals of advance in Renaissance historiography. Its passion for a return to old disciplines was submerged by its enthusiasm for man's new and growing powers. This enthusiasm was increased as evidence accumulated that among man's unique gifts belonged the capacity to increase his freedom and power indeterminately. Had not human institutions developed from crude and barbaric beginnings to their present proud estate? The nineteenth century added to this new certainty not only the assurance that nature itself was subject to growth but also the obvious achievements of applied science. The phenomenal technical advances of the century, outstripping the slow conquest of nature of all previous eras, seemed to be the final proof of the validity of modern man's new faith in history. The classical conception of time as a cycle of endless recurrences was finally overcome. Time was no longer a mystery which required explanation. It became the principle of interpretation by which the mystery of life was comprehended. History was no longer an enigma. It became the assurance of man's redemption from his every ill.

The modern age is variously described as an age of science or as an age of reason. Confidence in the power of reason, and particularly in the inductive and empirical strategy of the rational faculty, is indeed a characteristic of our age. But the classical ages also believed in the power and virtue of reason. Modern culture is distinguished by its confidence, both in the growing power of reason and in its capacity, when rightly disciplined, to assure the development of every human power and virtue.

The dominant note in modern culture is not so much confidence in reason as faith in history. The conception of a redemptive history informs the most diverse forms of modern culture.

The rationalist, Leibnitz, shared it with the romanticist, Herder. Kant's critical idealism was not so obviously informed by the new historical sense as the thought of Hegel, who had reinterpreted Platonism to conform to the historical consciousness of modernity; but Kant was as certain as Hegel of a movement of history toward increasing rationality. J. S. Mill's utilitarianism stood in sharp contradiction to Kant's ethics; but Mill agreed with Kant that history was moving toward a universal concord of life with life. The difference between the French Enlightenment's material-ism and the idealism of the German Enlightenment made no appreciable difference in the common historical optimism of both. The French physiocrats believed that progress would be assured by the removal of the irrelevancies of historical restraints from the operation of the laws of nature; while Comte thought it would be achieved by bringing social process under the control of an elite of social scientists. But this contrast between determinism and voluntarism (which is, incidentally, never composed in modern culture) had no influence upon the shared belief in progress. There is only a slight difference in optimism between the determi-nistic thought of Herbert Spencer and the modern voluntarism of John Dewey.

Even Karl Marx, who introduced a provisional historical catas-trophism to challenge the optimism of bourgeois life, did not shake the modern conception of a redemptive history basically. He saw in the process of historical development certain "dialecti-cal" elements not observed in bourgeois theories. He knew that there is disintegration as well as increasing integration in history; that there is death as well as growth. But he also believed that a new life and a new age would rise out of the death of an old one with dialectical necessity. Catastrophe was the certain prelude of redemption in his scheme of salvation. The ultimate similarity between Marxist and bourgeois optimism, despite the provisional catastrophism of the former, is, in fact, the most telling proof of the unity of modern culture. It is a unity which transcends war-ring social philosophies, conflict between which contributed to the refutation of a common hope.

The goal toward which history was presumably moving was variously defined. The most unreflective forms of historical optimism in the nineteenth century assumed that increasing physical comfort and well-being were the guarantee of every other form of advance. Sometimes the enlarging human community was believed to be developing inevitably toward a universal community, for "clans and tribes, long narrowly self-regarding, are finally enlarged and compacted into nations; and nations move inevitably, however slowly, into relations with one another, whose ultimate goal is the unification of mankind."[1] It may be recorded in passing that scarcely a single student in the modern era noted the marked difference between the task of unifying tribes, nations and empires and the final task of the unification of mankind. In the former case there is always some particular force of geography, language, common experience or the fear of a common foe which furnishes the core of cohesion. In the latter case unity must be achieved in defiance of the unique and particularistic forces of historical concretion.

Sometimes, as in H. G. Wells' *Outline of History*, the historical process is assumed to be moving toward the democratization, as well as the universalization, of the human community. The democratic culmination, toward which history was presumably moving was frequently defined in contradictory terms. Libertarians thought they saw a movement toward increasing liberty while equalitarians and collectivists thought they could discern a movement toward more intense social cohesion.

Nor was there agreement about the cause of historical advance. Social Darwinism as well as other forms of naturalism looked upon historical development as a mere extension of natural evolution. The Darwinists saw the guarantee of progress in the survival of the fittest. Others discerned a movement in both nature and history from consistent egoism to a greater and greater consideration of the interests of others.[2]

---

[1]Edmund Noble, *Purposive Evolution*, p. 418.

[2]Prince Kropotkin in *Mutual Aid* traced the development from limited mutual aid in the animal world to wider and wider extensions of mutuality. Leslie Stephens described an evolutionary development of conscience as the "gradual growth of social tissue." (*The Science of Ethics*, p. 120.)

W. K. Clifford equated an evolutionary development of the moral sense with the growth of a "tribal self." (*Lectures and Essays*. II, p. 110.)

More frequently historical development was regarded not so much as an extension of forces operative in nature as a negation of natural impulses through the growth of mind. The method of reason's triumph over the irrationalities of nature was, however, variously interpreted. The French Enlightenment assigned reason the primary function of discerning the "laws of nature" and of destroying man's abortive efforts to circumvent these laws. Comte, on the other hand, believed that a scientific political program would bring the irrational factors in man's common life under rational control. Condorcet believed that justice would triumph when universal education destroyed the advantage which the shrewd had over the simple. Or it was assumed that increasing rationality would gradually destroy the irrational (primarily religious) justifications of special privilege.[3] Or that increasing reason would gradually prompt all men to grant their fellowmen justice, the power of logic requiring that the interests of each individual be brought into a consistent scheme of value.[4] More recently the psychological sciences have hoped for the increasing control or elimination of self-regarding impulses and the extension of human sympathy through the rational control of man's subrational life.

Though modern culture is predominantly rationalistic, so that even naturalistic philosophies place their primary confidence in increasing rationality, the subordinate romantic distrust of reason must not be obscured. Romanticism in its most consistent form has a preference for the primitive, which implies a pessimistic estimate of the growth of civilization. Rousseau's dictum that men were born free and are now everywhere in chains led to a provisional pessimism; but this did not prevent him from elaborating a system of historical optimism, based on confidence in the possibility of bringing all competing wills into the concurrence of a general will. Bergson's distrust of reason likewise failed to arrest his optimistic conclusions about historical development. He placed his confidence in the growth of a mystical capacity, which would lift men from particular to universal loyalties.[5]

[3]This is the thesis of Robert Briffault's *Rational Evolution.*

[4]L. T. Hobhouse bases his confidence in progress upon this argument in *Principles of Social Justice, The Rational Good,* and *Development and Purpose.*

[5]*Cf.* Henri Bergson, *Two Sources of Religion and Morality.*

The fact that the prevailing mood of modern culture was able to transmute the original pessimism of romanticism into an optimistic creed proves the power of this mood. Only occasionally the original pessimism erupts in full vigor, as in the thought of a Schopenhauer or Nietzsche. The subjugation of romantic pessimism, together with the transmutation of Marxist catastrophism establishes historical optimism far beyond the confines of modern rationalism. Though there are minor dissonances the whole chorus of modern culture learned to sing the new song of hope in remarkable harmony. The redemption of mankind, by whatever means, was assured for the future. It was, in fact, assured by the future.

II

There were experiences in previous centuries which might well have challenged this unqualified optimism. But the expansion of man's power over nature proceeded at such a pace that all doubts were quieted, allowing the nineteenth century to become the "century of hope"[6] and to express the modern mood in its most extravagant terms. History, refusing to move by the calendar, actually permitted the nineteenth century to indulge its illusions into the twentieth. Then came the deluge. Since 1914 one tragic experience has followed another, as if history had been designed to refute the vain delusions of modern man.

The "laws" and tendencies of historical development proved in the light of contemporary experience to be much more complex than any one has supposed. Every new freedom represented a new peril as well as a new promise. Modern industrial society dissolved ancient forms of political authoritarianism; but the tyrannies which grew on its soil proved more brutal and vexatious than the old ones. The inequalities rooted in landed property were levelled. But the more dynamic inequalities of a technical society became more perilous to the community than the more static forms of uneven power. The achievement of individual liberty was one of the genuine advances of bourgeois society. But this society also created atomic individuals who, freed from the disciplines of the older organic communities, were lost in the mass; and became

6*Cf.* F.S. Marvin, *The Century of Hope.*

the prey of demagogues and charlatans who transmuted their individual anxieties and resentments into collective political power of demonic fury.

The development of instruments of communication and transportation did create a potential world community by destroying all the old barriers of time and space. But the new interdependence of the nations created a more perplexing problem than anyone had anticipated. It certainly did not prompt the nations forthwith to organize a "parliament of man and federation of the world." Rather it extended the scope of old international frictions so that a single generation was subjected to two wars of global dimensions. Furthermore the second conflict left the world as far from the goal of global peace as the first. At its conclusion the world's peace was at the mercy of two competing alliances of world savers, the one informed by the bourgeois and the other by the proletarian creed of world redemption. Thus the civil war in the heart of modern industrial nations, which had already brought so much social confusion into the modern world, was re-enacted in the strife between nations. The development of atomic instruments of conflict aggravated the fears not only of those who lacked such instruments, but of those who had them. The fears of the latter added a final ironic touch to the whole destiny of modern man. The possession of power has never annulled the fears of those who wield it, since it prompts them to anxiety over its possible loss. The possession of a phenomenal form of destructive power in the modern day has proved to be so fruitful of new fears that the perennial ambiguity of man's situation of power and weakness became more vividly exemplified, rather than overcome. Thus a century which was meant to achieve a democratic society of world-scope finds itself at its half-way mark uncertain about the possibility of avoiding a new conflict of such proportions as to leave the survival of mankind, or at least the survival of civilization, in doubt.

The tragic irony of this refutation by contemporary history of modern man's conception of history embodies the spiritual crisis of our age. Other civilizations have assumed their own indestructibility, usually indulging in pretensions of immortality in a "golden age," precisely when their ripeness was turning into over-ripeness and portents of their disintegration were becoming discernible. It remained for the culture of the Renaissance and Enlightenment to raise this *Hybris* of civilizations to a new and absurd height by claiming to have found the way of arresting the decay not merely of a particular civilization but of civilization as such. Was not the "scientific conquest of nature" a "sure method" by which the "wholesale permanent decay of civilization has become impossible"?[7] Had not the scientific method established the dominion of man over nature in place of "the dominion of man over the labor of others" which was the "shaky basis" of older civilizations?

Contemporary experience represents a *Nemesis* which is justly proportioned in its swiftness and enormity to the degree of *Hybris* which had expressed itself in modern life. In one century modern man had claimed to have achieved the dizzy heights of the mastery both of natural process and historical destiny. In the following century he is hopelessly enmeshed in an historical fate, threatening mutual destruction, from which he seems incapable of extricating himself. A word of Scripture fits the situation perfectly: "He that sitteth in the heavens shall laugh: the Lord shall have them in derision" (Psalms 2 : 4).

The modern experience belongs in the category of pathos or irony rather than tragedy, because contemporary culture has no vantage point of faith from which to understand the predicament of modern man. It is therefore incapable either of rising to a tragic defiance of destiny, as depicted in Greek drama, or of achieving a renewal of life through a contrite submission to destiny, as in Christian tragedy. Subsequent centuries (if, indeed, there be survivors capable of reflecting upon the meaning of the experience of this age) may discern in it the pathos characteristic of Thomas Hardy's novels. For the actors in the drama are enmeshed in an inscrutable fate, which either drives them to despair or for which they find false interpretations.

Most of the explanations of contemporary catastrophe are derived from principles of interpretation which were responsible for modern man's inability to anticipate the experiences which he

[7] John Dewey, in *International Journal of Ethics,* April 1916, p. 313.

now seeks to comprehend. A culture, rooted in historical optimism, naturally turns first of all to the concepts of "retrogression" and "reversion" to explain its present experience. Thus Nazism is interpreted as a "reversion to barbarism" or even as a "reversion to the cruelty of the Middle Ages." We are assured that mankind has no right to expect an uninterrupted ascent toward happiness and perfection. Comfort is drawn from the figure of a "spiral" development. This is usually accompanied by the assurance that no recession ever reaches the depth of previous ones and that each new "peak" achieves a height beyond those of the past. This spiral version of the concept of progress is hardly more adequate than the simpler version; for both the failures and achievements of advanced civilizations are incommensurable with those of simpler societies. To call them better or worse by comparison is almost meaningless. Insofar as comparisons can be made it is idle to regard the tyrannies and anarchies which result from the breakdown of an advanced and highly integrated civilization as preferable to the social confusion of more primitive societies.

An equally favored mode of reassurance is to take a long view of history, to enlarge upon the millennia of pre-historic barbarism which preceded the known, and comparatively brief, period of civilized life, and to express the hope that present misfortunes belong to the period of civilization's infancy which will be forgotten in the unimagined heights of perfection which will be achieved in the unimagined subsequent ages. So James Bryce wrote in the period of disillusionment, following the first world war: "Shaken out of that confident hope in progress . . . mankind must resume its efforts toward improvement in a chastened mood, . . . consoled by the reflection that it has taken a thousand years to emerge from savagery and less than half that time to rise above the shameless sensualities of the ancient world and the ruthless ferocity of the Dark Ages."[8]

A modern biologist seeks comfort in a similar logic: "When world wide wars, with their indescribable sufferings and horrors, brutalities and tyrannies shake one's faith in human progress, it is conforting to take a long view of cosmic evolution and remember

[8]*Modern Democracies,* Vol. II, p. 607 (1921).

that the longest wars are but a fraction of a second on the clock of life on earth, and that 'eternal process moving on' is not likely to stop today or tomorrow."[9]

These comforting assurances rest upon the dubious assumption that the "shameless sensualities" of the ancient world and the "ruthless ferocity" of the Dark Ages have no counterpart in modern life. The belief that human brutality is a vestigial remnant of man's animal or primitive past represents one of the dearest illusions of modern culture, to which men cling tenaciously even when every contemporary experience refutes it.

The appeal to future millennia of the world's history, in comparison with which past history is but a brief episode and its periods of conflict but seconds on the clock of time, is hardly reassuring when for instance the history of warfare in this brief episode is considered. For that history contains the development from partial and limited to total wars; and the evolution of means of combat from spears to atomic bombs. To be sure historical development contains creative movements as well as progress in means of destruction. But the fact that history contains such developments as progress in the lethal efficacy of our means of destruction and the increasing consistency of tyrannical governments must prove the vanity of our hope in historical development as such. The prospect of the extension of history into untold millennia must, if these facts are considered, sharpen, rather than assuage, man's anxiety about himself and his history.

A more favored explanation of present catastrophies is to hold the "cultural lag" responsible for them, which means to attribute them to the failure of man's social wisdom to keep pace with his technical advances. This explanation has the merit of being quite true as an interpretation of specific evils, arising from specific maladjustments between a culture and its social institutions, or between the economic and technical arrangements of an era and its political forms. It nevertheless hides a profound illusion with reference to the total situation.

One of the most potent causes of historical evil is the inability of men to bring their customs and institutions into conformity with new situations. Political institutions developed in a pastoral soci-

[9]Edward G. Conklin, *Man: Real and Ideal*, pp. 205–206.

ety maintain themselves stubbornly in an agararian economy; and agrarian institutions are projected into a commercial age. In a period of rapid technical advance these maladjustments are a source of great social confusion. It is obvious, for instance, that the sometimes extravagant individualism of the commercial age is not an adequate social philosophy for the intense social cohesion of a new industrial age; and that the national sovereignties of the past must be abridged to permit the growth of international political institutions, consonant with the economic interdependence of modern nations. All this is clear.

The error embodied in the theory of the cultural lag is the modern assumption that the "cultural lag" is due merely to the tardiness of the social sciences in achieving the same standards of objectivity and disinterestedness which characterize the natural sciences. This belief embodies the erroneous idea that man's knowledge and conquest of nature develops the wisdom and the technics required for the knowledge and the conquest of human nature.

It is man in the unity of his being who must come to terms with his fellowmen and, for that matter, with himself. Scientific knowledge of what human nature is and how it reacts to various given social situations will always be of service in refashioning human conduct. But ultimately the problems of human conduct and social relations are in a different category from the relations of physical nature. The ability to judge friend or foe with some degree of objectivity is, in the ultimate instance, a moral and not an intellectual achievement, since it requires the mitigation of fears and prejudices, envies and hatreds which represent defects, not of the mind, but of the total personality. Moreover, the ability to yield to the common good, to forego special advantages for a larger measure of social justice, to heal the breach between warring factions by forgiveness, or to acknowledge a common human predicament between disputants in a social situation, is the fruit of a social wisdom to which science makes only ancillary contributions. This type of wisdom involves the whole of man in the unity of his being. The modern belief that "scientific objectivity" may be simply extended from the field of nature to the field of history obscures the unity of the self which acts, and is acted upon, in history. It also obscures the ambiguity of the human self; for the self as the creature of history is the same self which must be the creator of history. The creaturely limitations which corrupt his actions as creator are, however, never the limitations of mere ignorance. The self as creator does not master the self as creature merely by the extension of scientific technics. The hope that everything recalcitrant in human behaviour may be brought under the subjection of the inclusive purposes of "mind" by the same technics which gained man mastery over nature is not merely an incidental illusion, prompted by the phenomenal achievements of the natural sciences. It is the culminating error in modern man's misunderstanding of himself. Thus the principle of comprehension by which modern culture seeks to understand our present failure belongs to the misunderstanding about man's life and history which contributed to that failure. The spiritual confusions arising from this misunderstanding constitute the cultural crisis of our age, beyond and above the political crisis in which our civilization is involved. . . .

The knowledge that "the world passeth away and the lusts thereof" and that every *civitas terrena* is a city of destruction does not, however, negate the permanent values which appear in the rise and fall of civilizations and cultures. A feudal civilization may be destroyed by its inability to incorporate the new dynamism of a commercial and industrial society. But there are qualities of organic community, including even the hierarchical organization of the community, in a feudal society, which transcend the fate of such a civilization. In the same manner a bourgeois society, though involved in a self-destructive individualism, also contributes to the emancipation of the individual in terms of permanent worth. There are thus facets of the eternal in the flux of time. From the standpoint of Biblical faith the eternal in the temporal flux is not so much a permanent structure of existence, revealed in the cycle of change, as it is a facet of the *Agape* of Christ. It is "love which abideth." An organic society may achieve a harmony of life with life without freedom. Insofar as it is without freedom it is not a perfect incarnation of *Agape*. But insofar as it is a harmony of life with life it is an imperfect symbol of the true *Agape*. A libertarian society may sacrifice community to the dignity of the individual. But insofar as it emancipates the individual from social restraints which are less than the restraints of love, it illustrates another facet of the full dimension of *Agape*. Thus the same civilizations which perish because they violate the law of love at some point may also contribute a deathless value insofar as they explicate the harmony of life with life intended in creation.

If this be so, the question arises why the process of history should not gradually gather up the timeless values and eliminate the worthless. Why should not history be a winnowing process in which truth is separated from falsehood; and the falsehood burned as chaff, while the wheat of truth is "gathered into the barn." In that case *die Weltgeschichte* would, after all, be *das Weltgericht*. There is one sense in which this is true. Yet this conception of history as its own judge is finally false. It is true in the sense that history is actually the story of man's developing freedom. Insofar as increasing freedom leads to harmonies of life with life within communities and between communities, in which the restraints and cohesions of nature are less determinative for the harmony than the initiative of men, a positive meaning must be assigned to growth in history. There is, certainly, positive significance in the fact that modern man must establish community in global terms or run the risk of having his community destroyed even on the level of the local village. To establish community in global terms requires the exercise of the ingenuity of freedom far beyond the responsibilities of men of other epochs, who had the support of natural forces, such as consanguinity, for their limited communities. The expansion of the perennial task of achieving a tolerable harmony of life with life under ever higher conditions of freedom and in ever wider frames of harmony represents the residual truth in modern progressive interpretations of history.

But this truth is transmuted into error very quickly if it is assumed that increasing freedom assures the achievement of the wider task. The perils of freedom rise with its promises, and the perils and promises are inextricably interwoven. The parable of the wheat and the tares expresses the Biblical attitude toward the possibilities of history exactly. The servants who desire to uproot the tares which have been sown among the wheat are forbidden to do so by the householder "lest while ye gather up the tares, ye root up also the wheat with them. Let both grow together until the harvest: and in the time of harvest I will say unto the reapers, Gather ye together first the tares, and bind them in bundles to burn them: but gather the wheat into my barn" (Matthew 13 : 29–30).

There is, in other words, no possibility of a final judgement within history but only at the end of history. The increase of human freedom over nature is like the advancing season which ripens both wheat and tares, which are inextricably intermingled. This simple symbol from the sayings of our Lord in the synoptics is supplemented in the eschatology of the Epistles, where it is Christ himself who becomes the judge at the final judgement of the world.

History, in short, does not solve the enigma of history. There are facets of meaning in it which transcend the flux of time. These give glimpses of the eternal love which bears the whole project of history. There is a positive meaning also in the ripening of love under conditions of increasing freedom; but the possibility that the same freedom may increase the power and destructiveness of self-love makes it impossible to find a solution for the meaning of history within history itself. Faith awaits a final judgement and a final resurrection. Thus mystery stands at the end, as well as at the beginning of the whole pilgrimage of man. But the clue to the mystery is the *Agape* of Christ. It is the clue to the mystery of Creation. "All things were made by him; and without him was not any thing made that was made" (John 1:3). It is the clue to the mystery of the renewals and redemptions within history, since wherever the divine mercy is discerned as within and above the wrath, which destroys all forms of self-seeking, life may be renewed, individually and collectively. It is also the clue to the final redemption of history. The antinomies of good and evil increase rather than diminish in the long course of history. Whatever provisional meanings there may be in such a process, it must drive men to despair when viewed ultimately, unless they have discerned the power and the mercy which overcomes the enigma of its end.

The whole history of man is thus comparable to his individual life. He does not have the power and the wisdom to overcome the ambiguity of his existence. He must and does increase his freedom, both as an individual and in the total human enterprise; and his creativity is enhanced by the growth of his freedom. But this freedom also tempts him to deny his mortality and the growth of freedom and power increases the temptation. But evils in history are the consequence of this pretension. Confusion follows upon man's effort to complete his life by his own power and solve its enigma by his own wisdom. Perplexities, too simply solved, produce despair. The Christian faith is the apprehension of the divine love and power which bears the whole human pilgrimage, shines through its enigmas and antinomies and is finally and definitively revealed in a drama in which suffering love gains triumph over sin and death. This revelation does not resolve all perplexities; but it does triumph over despair, and leads to the renewal of life from self-love to love.

Man, in both his individual life and in his total enterprise, moves from a limited to a more extensive expression of freedom over nature. If he assumes that such an extension of freedom insures and increases emancipation from the bondage of self, he increases the bondage by that illusion. Insofar as the phenomenal increase in human power in a technical age has created that illusion, it has also involved our culture in the profound pathos of disappointed hopes, caused by false estimates of the glory and the misery of man.

ARNOLD TOYNBEE

The World and the West

We may begin by reminding ourselves of a general phenomenon which came to our notice in the last chapter when we were
taking a comparative view of our Western civilization's two successive assaults upon China and Japan. We saw that, on the first
occasion, the West tried to induce the Far Eastern peoples to
adopt the Western way of life in its entirety, including its religion
as well as its technology, and that this attempt did not succeed.
And then we saw that, in the second act of the play, the West
offered to the same Far Eastern peoples a secularized excerpt
from the Western civilization in which religion had been left out
and technology, instead of religion, had been made the central
feature; and we observed that this technological splinter, which
had been flaked off from the religious core of our civilization
towards the end of the seventeenth century, did succeed in push-
ing its way into the life of a Far Eastern Society that had
previously repulsed an attempt to introduce the Western way of
life *en bloc*—technology and all, including religion.

Here we have an example of something that seems often to
happen when the culture-ray of a radioactive civilization hits a

From *The World and the West* by Arnold J. Toynbee. Copyright 1953 by
Oxford University Press, Inc. Reprinted by permission. Pp. 277–281, 287–288,
292–298.

foreign body social. The assaulted foreign body's resistance diffracts the culture-ray into its component strands, just as a light-ray is diffracted into the spectrum by the resistance of a prism. In optics we also know that some of the light-strands in the spectrum have a greater penetrative power than others, and we have already seen that it is the same with the component strands of a culture-ray. In the West's impact on the Far East, the technological strand in the radiation of the Western civilization has overcome a resistance by which the religious strand has been repelled; and this difference in the penetrative power of a religious and a technological culture-strand is not a phenomenon that is peculiar to the history of the relations between these two particular civilizations. We have stumbled here upon an instance of one of the "laws" of cultural radiation.

When a travelling culture-ray is diffracted into its component stands—technology, religion, politics, art, and so on—by the resistance of a foreign body social upon which it has impinged, its technological strand is apt to penetrate faster and farther than its religious strand; and this law can be formulated in more general terms. We can say that the penetrative power of a strand of cultural radiation is usually in inverse ratio to this strand's cultural value. A trivial strand arouses less resistance in the assaulted body social than is aroused by a crucial strand, because the trivial strand does not threaten to cause so violent or so painful a disturbance of the assaulted body's traditional way of life. This automatic selection of the most trivial elements in a radioactive culture for the widest dissemination abroad is obviously an unfortunate rule of the game of cultural intercourse; but this premium on triviality is not the game's worst point. The very process of diffraction, which is of the essence of the game, threatens to poison the life of the society whose body social is being penetrated by the divers strands of a diffracted culture-ray.

Analogies taken from physics and medicine may be used to illustrate this point. Since our discovery of the trick of splitting the atom, we have learnt to our cost that the particles composing an atom of some inoffensive element cease to be innocuous and become dangerously corrosive so soon as they have been split off from the orderly society of particles of which an atom is constituted, and have been sent flying by themselves on independent careers of their own. We have learnt, too—not to our own cost in this case, but to the cost of the once secluded surviving representatives of Primitive Man—that a disease which is a mild one for us, because it has been rife among us so long that we have developed an effective resistance to it, may prove deadly to South Sea Islanders who have been exempt from it before being suddenly exposed to it by the arrival among them of its European carriers.

A loose strand of cultural radiation, like a loose electron or a loose contagious disease, may prove deadly when it is disengaged from the system within which it has been functioning hitherto and is set free to range abroad by itself in a different milieu. In its original setting, this culture-strand or bacillus or electron was restrained from working havoc because it was kept in order by its association with other components of a pattern in which the divers participants were in equilibrium. In escaping from its original setting, the liberated particle, bacillus, or culture-strand will not have changed its nature; but the same nature will produce a deadly effect, instead of a harmless one, now that the creature has broken loose from its original associations. In these circumstances, "one man's meat" can become "another man's poison."

In the set of encounters between the world and the West which is the subject of this book, there is a classical example of the mischief that an institution can do when it is prised loose from its original social setting and is sent out into the world, conquering and to conquer, all by itself. During the last century and a half we have seen our Late Modern Western political institution of "national states" burst the bounds of its birthplace in Western Europe and blaze a trail of persecution, eviction, and massacre as it has spread abroad into Eastern Europe, South-West Asia, and India— all of them regions where "national states" were not part and parcel of an indigenous social system but were an exotic institution which was deliberately imported from the West, not because it had been found by experimentation to be suitable to the local conditions of these non-Western worlds, but simply because the West's political power had given the West's political institutions an irrational yet irresistible prestige in non-Western eyes.

The havoc which the application of this Western institution of "national states" has worked in these regions where it is an exotic import is incomparably greater than the damage that the same institution has done in Britain, France, and the other West European countries in which it has been, not an artificially introduced innovation, but a spontaneous native growth.

We can see why the same institution has had strikingly different effects in these two different social environments. The institution of "national states" has been comparatively harmless in Western Europe for the same reason that accounts for its having originated there; and that is because, in Western Europe, it corresponds to the local relation between the distribution of languages and the alinement of political frontiers. In Western Europe, people speaking the same language happen, in most cases, to be huddled together in a single continuous and compact block of territory with a fairly well defined linguistic boundary separating it from the similarly compact domains of other languages; and, in a region where, as here, the languages are thus distributed in the pattern of a patchwork quilt, the linguistic map provides a convenient basis for the political map, and "national states" are therefore natural products of the social milieu. Most of the domains of the historic states of Western Europe do, in fact, coincide approximately with homogeneous patches of the linguistic map; and this coincidence has come about, for the most part, undesignedly. The West European peoples have not been acutely conscious of the process by which their political containers have been moulded on linguistic lasts; and, accordingly, the spirit of nationalism has been, on the whole, easy-going in its West European homeland. In West European national states, linguistic minorities who have found themselves on the wrong side of a political frontier have in most cases shown loyalty, and been treated with consideration, because their coexistence with the majority speaking "the national language" as fellow citizens of the same commonwealth has been an historical fact which has not been deliberately brought about by anyone and which has therefore been taken for granted by everyone. . . .

Our inquiry will have made it evident that the reception of a foreign culture is a painful as well as a hazardous undertaking;

and the victim's instinctive repugnance to innovations that threaten to upset his traditional way of life makes the experience all the worse for him; for, by kicking against the pricks, he diffracts the impinging foreign culture-ray into its component strands; he then gives a grudging admission to the most trivial, and therefore least upsetting, of these poisonous splinters of a foreign way of life, in the hope of being able to get off with no further concessions than just that; and then, as one thing inevitably leads to another, he finds himself compelled to admit the rest of the intruding culture piecemeal. No wonder that the victim's normal attitude towards an intrusive alien culture is a self-defeating attitude of opposition and hostility.

In the course of our survey we have had occasion to notice some of the statesmen in non-Western countries hit by the West who have had the rare vision to see that a society which is under fire from the radiation of a more potent foreign culture must either master this foreign way of life or perish. The figures of Peter the Great, Selīm III, Mahmūd II, Mehmed 'Alī, Mustafā Kemāl, and "the Elder Statesmen" of Japan in the Meiji Era have passed before our eyes. This positive and constructive response to the challenge of cultural aggression is a proof of statesmanship because it is a victory over natural inclinations. The natural response is the negative one of the oyster who closes his shell, the tortoise who withdraws into his carapace, the hedgehog who rolls himself up into a spiky ball, or the ostrich who hides his head in the sand, and there are classical examples of this alternative reaction in the histories of both Russia's and Islam's encounters with the West.

The policy of learning how to fight an aggressive alien civilization with its own weapons will arouse deep misgivings in conservative minds. Are not your Peters and your Mustafā Kemāls really selling the fort under pretex of bringing its defences up to date? Is not the right retort to the intrusion of an alien culture a resolute determination to boycott the accursed thing? If we scrupulously obey every jot and tittle of the holy law that has been laid upon us by the God of our fathers, will He not be moved to put forth the almighty power of His right arm for our defence against our infidel enemies? In Russia this was the reaction of the

Old Believers, who suffered martyrdom for the sake of minute, and in foreign eyes trifling, points of ecclesiastical ritual; and in the Islamic world this was the reaction of the Wahhābīs, Sanūsīs, Idrīsīs, Mahdists, and other puritanical sects who came charging out of the desert on God's war-path against apostate Osmanlis, who, in the fanatics' eyes, had betrayed Islam by going the Western way.

Muhammad Ahmad, the Sudanese fanatic, is the antithesis of Peter the Russian technocrat; but neither the mastering of a new-fangled alien technology nor a zeal for the preservation of a traditional way of life is the last word in reply to the challenge of an assulting alien civilization. If we are to read what this last word is, we must look ahead to a chapter of the story which, in the unfinished history of the world's encounter with the West, is today still hidden in the future. We can supply this missing chapter if we turn to the history of the world's encounter with the Greeks and Romans; for, in the record of this episode, the scroll of history has already been unrolled from beginning to end, so that the whole of this older book now lies open for our inspection. Our future can perhaps be deciphered in this record of a Graeco-Roman past. Let us see what we can make of this Graeco-Roman record. . . .

The World of the Greeks and the Romans

. . . Of course I am not meaning to suggest that we can cast a horoscope of our own future by observing what happened in Graeco-Roman history beyond this point, where our own record breaks off, and then mechanically translating this Graeco-Roman record into modern Western terms. History does not automatically repeat itself; and the most that any Graeco-Roman oracle can do for us is to reveal one among a number of alternative possible future denouements of our own drama. In our case the chances may well be against the plot's working out to its Graeco-Roman conclusion. It is conceivable that we Westerners and our non-Western contemporaries may give the course of our encounter with each other some quite different turn which has no counter-part in Graeco-Roman history. In peering into the future we are fumbling in the dark, and we must be on our guard against imagining that we can map out the hidden road ahead. All the same, it would be foolish not to make the most of any glimmer of light that hovers before our eyes; and the light reflected upon our future by the mirror of past Graeco-Roman history is at any rate the most illuminating gleam that is visible to us.

With these counsels of caution in our minds, let us now go on turning the pages of the book of Graeco-Roman history till we come to the picture of the Graeco-Roman world half-way through the second century after Christ. When we compare this with the picture of the same world two hundred years earlier, we shall perceive at once that in the interval there has been a change for the better here which unfortunately has had no parallel in our Western history up to date. In the last century B.C. the Graeco-Roman world had been racked by revolutions, wars, and rumours of wars, and had been seething with tumult and violence, quite as feverishly as our Western world is today; but midway through the second century after Christ we find peace reigning from the Ganges to the Tyne. The whole of this vast area, stretching from India to Britain, through which the Graeco-Roman civilization has been propagated by force of arms, is now divided between no more than three states, and these three are managing to live side by side with a minimum of friction. The Roman Empire round the shore of the Mediterranean, the Parthian Empire in 'Irāq and Iran, and the Kushan Empire in Central Asia, Afghanistan and Hindustan, cover the whole of the Graeco-Roman world between them; and, though the makers and masters of these three empires are all non-Greek in origin, they are nevertheless all "Philhellenes," as they are proud to call themselves: that is to say, they consider it to be their duty and their privilege to foster the Greek form of culture and to cherish the self-governing municipalities in which this Greek way of life is being kept alive.

Let us look into the hearts and minds of the millions of Greeks and Romans and the many more millions of Hellenized and semi-Hellenized ex-Orientals and ex-barbarians who are living under the shelter of a second-century Roman-Parthian-Kushan peace. The waters of war and revolution which had gone over the souls of this generation's great-great-grandparents have now ebbed away, and the nightmare of that time of troubles has long since ceased to be a living memory. Social life has been stablized by constructive statesmanship; and, though the settlement has fallen far short of the ideals of social justice, it is tolerable even for the peasantry and the proletariat, while for all classes it is indisputably preferable to the Ishmaelitish anarchy to which it has put a long overdue end. Life now is more secure than it was in the preceding age; but for this very reason it is also more dull. Like humane anaesthetists, a Caesar and an Arsaces and a Kanishka have taken the sting out of those once burning economic and political questions that, in a now already half-forgotten past, were the salt as well as the bane of human life. The benevolent action of efficient authoritarian governments has undesignedly created a spiritual vacuum in human souls.

How is this spiritual vacuum going to be filled? That is the grand question in the Graeco-Roman world in the second century after Christ; but the sophisticated civil servants and philosophers are still unaware that any such question is on the agenda. The people who have read the signs of the times and have taken action in the light of these indications are the obscure missionaries of half-a-dozen Oriental religions. In the long-drawn-out encounter between the world and the Greeks and Romans, these preachers of strange religions have gently stolen the initiative out of Greek and Roman hands—so gently that those hard hands have felt no touch and, so far, have taken no alarm. Yet, all the same, the tide has turned in the Greeks' and Romans' trial of strength with the world. The Graeco-Roman offensive has spent its force; a counter-offensive is on its way; but this counter-movement is not yet recognized for what it is, because it is being launched on a different plane. The offensive has been military, political, and economic; the counter-offensive is religious. This new religious movement has before it a prodigious future, as time is going to show. What are the secrets of its coming success? There are three on which we can put our finger.

One factor that, in the second century after Christ, is favouring the rise and spread of the new religions is a weariness of the clash of cultures. We have watched the Orientals responding to the challenge of a radioactive Greek culture along two antithetical lines. There have been statesmen of Herod the Great's school, whose prescription for living in a Graeco-Roman cultural climate has been to acclimatize oneself, and there have been fanatics whose prescription has been to ignore the change of climate and to go on behaving as though this change had not occurred. After an exhaustive trial of both these strategies, fanaticism has discredited itself by turning out to be disastrous, while the Herodian policy has discredited itself by turning out to be unsatisfying. Whichever of the two alternative strategies has been followed, this cultural warfare has led nowhere; and the moral of this anticlimax is that no single human culture can make good its conceited claim to be a spiritual talisman. Disillusioned minds and disappointed hearts are now ready for a gospel that will rise above these barren cultural claims and counter-claims. And here is the opportunity for a new society, in which there shall be neither Scythian nor Jew nor Greek, neither bond nor free, neither male nor female, but in which all shall be one in Christ Jesus—or in Mithras, Cybele, Isis, or one of the bodhisattvas, an Amitabha or perhaps an Avalokita.

An ideal of human fraternity that will overcome the clash of cultures is thus the first secret of the new religions' success, and the second secret is that these new societies, which are open to all human beings, with no discrimination between cultures, classes, or sexes, also bring their human members into a saving fellowship with a superhuman being; for the lesson that human nature without God's grace is not enough has by now been graven deep on the hearts of a generation that has seen the tragedy of a time of troubles followed by the irony of an oecumenical peace.

At least two breeds of human gods have now been tried and found wanting. The deified militarist has been a flagrant scandal. Alexander, as the Tyrrhenian pirate told him to his face in the story as we have it from Saint Augustine, would have been called not a god but a gangster if he had done what he did with a couple of accomplices instead of doing it with a whole army. And what about the deified policeman? Augustus, now, has made himself into a policeman by liquidating all his fellow gangsters, and we are grateful to him for that; but, when we are required to register our gratitude by worshipping this reformed gangster as a god, we cannot comply with much conviction or enthusiasm; and yet our hearts are hungry for a divinity that we can worship in spirit and in truth.

In the gods who have made their epiphany in the new religions, we are at last in the presence of divinities to whom we can devote ourselves with all our heart and mind and strength. Mithras will lead us as our captain. Isis will nurse us as our mother. Christ has emptied Himself of His divine power and glory to become incarnate as a man and to suffer death upon the cross for our sake. And for our sake likewise a bodhisattva who has reached the threshold of Nirvāna has refrained from taking the last step into bliss. This heroic pathfinder has deliberately condemned himself to go on haunting the sorrowful treadmill of existence for aeons upon aeons more; and he has made this extreme sacrifice for the love of fellow sentient beings whose feet he can guide into the way of salvation so long as he pays the huge price of himself remaining sentient and suffering.

These were the appeals of the new religions to a majority of mankind who, in the Graeco-Roman world in the age of the imperial peace, were weary and heavy laden—as indeed they are at all times and places. But what about the Greek and Roman dominant minority that had devastated the world by conquering and plundering it, and were now patrolling the ruins as self-commissioned gendarmes? "They make a desert and call it peace" is the verdict on their handiwork that one of their own men of letters has put into the mouth of one of their barbarian victims. How were sophisticated and cynical Greek and Roman masters of the world going to respond to the challenge of the world's counter-offensive on the religious plane which was the world's answer to its rulers' previous offensive on the plane of war and politics?

If we look into these Greek and Roman hearts in the generation of Marcus Aurelius, we find a spiritual vacuum here also; for these earlier conquerors of the world, like us their present Western counterparts, had long ago discarded their ancestral religion. The way of life which they had chosen for themselves, and had been offering to all Orientals and barbarians whom they had

brought within the range of Greek cultural influence, was a
secular way in which the intellect has been conscripted to do duty
for the heart by working out philosophies that were to take
religion's place. These philosophies, which were to have set the
mind free, had bound the soul to the sorrowful wheel of natural
law. "Up and down, to and fro, round and round: this," the
philosopher-emperor Marcus confessed to himself, "is the mono-
tonous and meaningless rhythm of the Universe. A man of average intelligence who has arrived at the age of forty years will
have experienced everything that has been and is and is to
come."

This disillusioned Greek and Roman dominant minority was, in
fact, suffering from the same spiritual starvation as the majority
of contemporary mankind, but the new religions which were now
being offered to all men and women without respect of persons
would have stuck in a philosopher's throat if the missionary had
not sugared the strange pill for him; and so, for the sake of
accomplishing their last and hardest task of converting a Greek-
educated die-hard core of a pagan public, the new religions did
clothe themselves in divers forms of Greek dress. All of them,
from Buddhism to Christianity inclusive, presented themselves
visually in a Greek style of art, and Christianity took the further
step of presenting itself intellectually in terms of Greek philosophy.

This, then, was the last chapter in the history of the world's
encounter with the Greeks and Romans. After the Greeks and
Romans had conquered the world by force of arms, the world
took its conquerors captive by converting them to new religions
which addressed their message to all human souls without
discriminating between rulers and subjects or between Greeks,
Orientals, and barbarians. Is something like this historic denoue-
ment of the Graeco-Roman story going to be written into the
unfinished history of the world's encounter with the West? We
cannot say, since we cannot foretell the future. We can only see
that something which has actually happened once, in another
episode of history, must at least be one of the possibilities that lie
ahead of us.

Debates with Historians

To survey history as a whole, to discover trends in its movement, to seek out its meaning—Professor Toynbee is not the first
to undertake the attempt. He joins the company of St. Augustine
and Bossuet, Condorcet, Hegel, Marx, Buckle, Wells, Spengler;
nor is he the least among them. . . .

His work is intended to be a comparative study of civilizations
as a basis for general conceptions about history. Civilizations are
for him the real units of history, not States, which he is wont to
indicate contemptuously as "parochial," or nations, whose hyper-
trophied self-consciousness, under the description "nationalism,"
he detests. . . .

I have a feeling that I am stating the obvious. Yet when you
read *A Study of History* you will be struck by the insistence with
which the eloquent author asserts and repeats that he is conducting an empirical exploration, and that the conclusions at which

Pieter Geyl, *Debates with Historians* (New York: Meridian Books, 1958), pp.
109–110 (reprinted by permission of the Journal of the History of Ideas);
161–164 (reprinted by permission of the Virginia Quarterly Review); 179–180
(reprinted from Pieter Geyl's "From Ranke to Toynbee: Five Lectures on
Historians and Historiographical Problems," *Smith College Studies in History*,
vol. XXXIX, with the permission of Smith College); 192–195 (reprinted by
permission of the Journal of the History of Ideas).

he arrives, the whole system which he develops, his discovery and definition of laws by which the movement of civilizations is governed, all spring unaided from facts, facts scientifically observed and scientifically connected.

Now I contend that his conception of what an historical fact really is, of what an historical fact is worth, of what can be done with it, is open to very grave objections. Professor Toynbee does not like professional historians; he is inclined to deal somewhat contemptuously with them. Their perpetually critical attitude of mind and their eternal scepticism make him impatient. I am of course, as the French would put it, preaching for my own parish, but I can't help thinking that it is an altogether precious thing—a bracing thing that our civilization cannot do without—that the professional historian should preserve his scruples and his humility with respect to his subject, that he should be aware of the limits set to his knowledge, and that he should prefer his ignorance and his doubt to attractive but facile generalizations.

I don't mean that the historian should (as he is sometimes advised) stick to the facts. The facts are there to be used. Combinations, presentations, theories, are indispensable if we want to understand. But the historian should proceed cautiously in using the facts for these purposes. It goes without saying that he should try to ascertain the facts as exactly as possible; but the important thing is that he should remain conscious, even then, of the element of arbitrariness, of subjectivity, that necessarily enters into all combinations of facts, if only because one has to begin by selecting them; while next, one has to order them according to an idea which must, in part at least, be conceived in one's own mind.

I am quite ready to admit that academic historiography often sins by employing too much caution. This sometimes leads to a shrinking from the use of that precious gift of the imagination. Academic historians do not perhaps always sufficiently remember the great task of history, which is not, after all, meant to be a plaything for scholars in the seclusion of their study, but rather has a great social function to fulfill. I admit all this, and up to a point I can sympathize with Toynbee's impatience. Yet I believe that the scholarly caution of which I spoke is also one of the high duties of the historian and the essential condition of his usefulness.

Toynbee, with his immense learning, has a multitude of historical illustrations at his fingers' ends at every turn of his argument,
and he discourses with never-failing brilliance and never-failing
confidence on careers and personalities of statesmen or thinkers,
on tendencies, movements of thought, social conditions, wars,
customs of all countries and of all ages. Now the critical reader
will feel that each single one of his cases might give rise to
discussion. Each could be represented in a slightly or markedly
different way so as no longer to substantiate his argument. They
are not facts: they are subjective presentations of facts; they are
combinations or interpretations of facts. As the foundations of an
imposing superstructure of theory, they prove extraordinarily
shifting and shaky, and this in spite of the dexterity and assurance
with which Toynbee handles them.

To me it seems that all these large syntheses of history (and I
include Sorokin's) are vitiated by an insufficient appreciation of
the infinite complexity, of the many-sidedness, of the irreducible
variety of the life of mankind in all its aspects, which is after all
the stuff of which history is made. This applies with particular
force when an attempt is made to establish the laws governing the
cultural life of mankind.

The great Dutch historian Huizinga, who died in the last year
of the war, once wrote that the height of a civilization cannot be
measured. To me this seems a wise saying. It implies that civilizations cannot with any certainty be divided into higher and lower.
Toynbee's rigid classification of the successive stages of one and
the same civilization in a period of growth, followed after a
breakdown by a period of disintegration, remains to me, after
reading the many hundreds of brilliant pages in which he tries to
explain and to describe it, utterly incomprehensible. To judge a
civilization, or one particular stage of a civilization, steadily, and
to judge it whole, is a task which I think will always be beyond
the powers of the human intellect. We speak glibly—and I have
done so myself and shall no doubt do so again—of a golden age,
or of an age of decadence. In fact when one studies a golden age
in any detail one is struck by signs of corruption or weakness or
distress, at least equaling those which frighten us in our own time.
On the other hand, no age of decadence in history is without the

redeeming features of effort or of new birth. But to measure the one set of factors against the other is what the historian can never do with any certainty.

It is sometimes thought that we are beset by these difficulties only when facing the mystery of our own time. The historian has before him something that is completed, something that can be turned around and around on the dissecting table. What can help him in his analysis to reach a final verdict, so it is imagined, is that he knows the outcome. Surely that must be a sufficient indication of the trend of the period he is studying? No doubt the historian is often guided by the outcome in his judgments, and he cannot neglect the evidence of the outcome. But to think that it will solve all his riddles for him is to fall into a very dangerous delusion. The factors by which the outcome was brought about are numerous, and they are again dissimilar. How shall one decide whether it was the purely material factors that were decisive? One can guess, one can have one's personal conviction; one cannot prove.

Toynbee, no doubt, tries to simplify the problem by contending that the life of a civilization is completely self-reliant, that its fate is governed by spiritual forces alone. I am far from being an adherent of historic materialism, but this exclusive spiritualism is more than I can swallow. Toynbee elaborately tries to prove, for instance, that no civilization has ever been broken down by outside violence. It is always by the spiritual shortcomings of the civilization itself that the breakdown is brought about. The argument is ingenious, but utterly unconvincing. If the thesis were true, the problem for the historian would still be staggering in its complexity, but it would be simplified. If one has to reject the thesis, as I do reject it, one can say only the more positively that the historian cannot fix the past in an unshakable pattern that will be valid for everyone, and from which conclusions as to the future can be drawn.

I need not, I trust, explain that I am not arguing against history as being of no use for the present. I believe, with Burckhardt, that, although it does not yield lessons for the immediate occasion, its study can make us wiser. And let me say that by *us* I do not mean the professional historians particularly; I mean the community in whose midst history is constantly being studied and written. I believe in the indispensable value of historical insight for civilized society. But we must not expect of history what history cannot possibly give—certainty. I do not quarrel with Toynbee when he soars above the ground of history where we others plod; the spectacle enthralls me even when I remain unconvinced. I admire the sweep of his imagination; I feel warmed by the glow of his enthusiasm; I am ready to regard his confessions of faith as significant manifestations in the struggle of minds that constitutes the cultural life of our time. But I enter my *caveat* when the great work is presented to the public as a work of scientific thought. As a prophet, as a poet, Toynbee is remarkable, and nobody will grudge him his appeals to history; one can only feel the liveliest admiration for his historical knowledge and for the inexhaustible picturesqueness and ingenuity with which he draws upon it. But when he pretends to be conducting a severely logical argument and builds up a system in so many stages and parts supposed to be based on a strictly empirical investigation, then I feel I must demur.

And the more so as it all leads to a conclusion that seems to me a dangerous one. Be converted or perish, Toynbee tells us; and he says it as if speaking with the authority of history behind him. But history does not warrant any such dilemma. Only the mystic will read into it the promise of a mystical salvation. To the rest of us it does not convey a message of despair. ... I am thinking now particularly of a review written by a professor of the Catholic University of Nymegen, of the Dutch volume in which, in 1950, my original Toynbee criticism was reissued. Professor Rogier, who is a faithful Catholic and a stimulating historical thinker, begins by observing that many of his co-religionists will not admit any criticism of Toynbee, because they are so profoundly impressed with his message, the message of salvation through Christ. But, says Rogier, this does not alter the fact that Toynbee offers as the result of empiricism what is purely apriorism; and even though I know, through God's revelation supported by infallible authority, that his apriori is in a general sense true, it is not, and it must not be represented as, a fact deduced from earthly data. And Rogier appeals to Bossuet, the great French Catholic writer, who stated, three centuries ago, that the concatenation of events which is History is ruled by God's secret decrees. The historian cannot trace that concatenation by his investigations. What he investigates are the ways of men, the acts determined by such freedom of decision as is left to human beings. "How the action of our liberty," said Bossuet, "is comprehended within the decrees of Divine Providence, remains hidden to us mortals." The system which Toynbee has constructed (I am still quoting or summarizing Rogier) may be intended to support divine truth. But it attempts to do so by presumptuously arranging verifiable facts as if the mystery of God's plan could thereby be solved. To show the insufficiency of that method, to knock away the structure of argument from under the conclusion, is a service rendered to intellectual honesty; nor does it touch the conclusion in so far as that is valuable to Christians, because in fact the ultimate truth rests upon a different foundation altogether.

I can gladly accept the alliance of the Catholic scholar. Part of his argument I should, certainly, state in different terms. But I am glad to find the method of Toynbee rejected, on the same ground which I advanced myself, by a man to whom the message conveys a real meaning. I am glad, because it shows that the laws of rational criticism can bridge a gulf which would be fatal to the unity of our civilization if it made an absolute separation between us.

That Toynbee cannot claim to be outside the jurisdiction of those laws should at any rate be self-evident. He is himself eager to assert that he lives by their light. To say that it is this which I find irritating in his work is really doing less than justice to the gravity of the case. Spengler, who openly proclaimed his contempt for those laws, was less of a danger to the great principle represented by them than is the man who pays them lip service but in fact uses them as a subterfuge to foist upon an anxious public his fanciful construction. Toynbee's system may not be as offensive as Spengler's in its political implications, but it is essentially no less irrational and aprioristic. By presenting it under the guise of scientific method and empiricism he not only revolts the scholar in me but he rouses me to protest, because I believe that clear thinking is perhaps the most crying need of our distracted world. . . .

Toynbee loves to talk about humility; "a contrite humility the first of the Christian virtues," he reminds us on the very last page of his Part on the Prospects. He had rejected Mr. Wright's plea for a recognition of the Christian religion as (to use Toynbee's own words) "possessing a monopoly of the Divine Light," and he rejected it on the ground that in making such a claim, "a church seems to me guilty of hybris." But in making the claim on behalf of the four higher religions collectively, or on behalf of his own personal conviction supported by ten volumes of eloquent and biased interpretation of history, it seems to me that he makes himself no less guilty of hybris. . . . When a man comes to the past with a compelling vision, a principle, or dogma, of such magnitude and emotional potence as Toynbee's unity in the love of God; with a system which causes him to reduce the multitudinous movement of history to one single, divinely inspired current, and to judge civilizations and generations by one single criterion, rejecting most of them, and incidentally his own, as unimportant— that man can write a work full of color and striking theories, glowing with conviction and eloquence, but no history. The *Study of History* is no history. The Student of History, as Toynbee calls himself, may know more of history than I shall ever do, but he is no historian. He is a prophet.

5

MORALITY AND HISTORY

The quest for meaning in history has been largely abandoned in our time, and for reasons we have already described. It should be noted further that the meaning sought was always, either overtly or covertly, a moral one. Accordingly, do we declare that history is without morality? Karl R. Popper would answer yes, history has no moral content except for what we, like others before us, have lent it. Is there no possibility, then, of making moral judgments in history? Here the answers are as various as the positions men adopt toward those in public life. If history, like social criticism, depends on the questions we ask ourselves, then it follows that our values play a large part in forming our historical judgments. Tolstoy despaired of finding morality in history. Others, persuaded of the truth of traditional Christianity, would find God's own morality in history. They might insist, however, that since we are all sinners we have no business judging others. To do so, moreover, might encourage a moral lassitude that permits us to rest comfortably on finding others guiltier than we are.

To any such Christian or non-Christian determinism, Isaiah Berlin has a reply. Having argued earlier that history

is life as we ordinarily know it, though defined and interpreted, he now argues further that we are required to
judge in the ordinary circumstances of life. Similarly, we
are not merely permitted but obliged to judge past events
and people. In the matter of morality history is nothing if
not the actions of people as we customarily describe
them—good or bad. We ask of the dead only what we ask
of the living when we form our judgments of their behavior.

There is a subtle difference between the arguments of
Berlin and those of Jacob Burckhardt. Whereas Berlin
thinks the judgments we bring to history are the traditional
ones, Burckhardt concludes that it is history that has
shaped our moral judgments, and that the study of history
allows us to refine them. To refer to Ortega once again,
"Man, in a word, has no nature; what he has is history."
The question of moral judgment becomes irrelevant when
we realize that we come to moral knowledge through the
study of history. Such knowledge is in part of men, but
more importantly of institutions, which require in this case
not so much that we judge them as that we understand
them if we are to make a better world.

Focusing on an institution such as the state, is of central
concern to contemporary scholarship and relates directly to
the problem of morality and history. So far as we care to
change institutions, the study of history may provide us not
with some grand design but with a grand intention to do so.
Armed with that purpose, and summarizing what we have
said before, history will equip us to stand prepared for the
future, though not to predict it. In this way history can be
said to have human value as distinguished from mere
utility. The efforts to find a moral meaning to history, either
immanent or transcendental, are countered by the assertion
of many historians that it is we who supply a meaning to
history by supplying one first to ourselves, and we create
one for ourselves in large part through the study of
history.

KARL R. POPPER

Has History Any Meaning?

History has no meaning, I contend. But this contention does not imply that all we can do about it is to look aghast at the history of political power, or that we must look on it as a cruel joke. For we can interpret it, with an eye to those problems of power politics whose solution we choose to attempt in our time. We can interpret the history of power politics from the point of view of our fight for the open society, for a rule of reason, for justice, freedom, equality, and for the control of international crime. Although history has no ends, we can impose these ends of ours upon it; and *although history has no meaning, we can give it a meaning.*

It is the problem of nature and convention which we meet here again. Neither nature nor history can tell us what we ought to do. Facts, whether those of nature or those of history, cannot make the decision for us, they cannot determine the ends we are going to choose. It is we who introduce purpose and meaning into nature and into history. Men are not equal; but we can decide to fight for equal rights. Human institutions such as the state are not

From *The Open Society and Its Enemies,* by Karl R. Popper (Vol. II, Princeton University Press, 4th rev. ed., 1963) and Routledge and Kegan Paul, 5th ed., 1966). Reprinted by permission of the author, Princeton University Press, and Routledge and Kegal Paul Ltd. The author's footnotes have been omitted.

rational, but we can decide to fight to make them more rational. We ourselves and our ordinary language are, on the whole, emotional rather than rational; but we can try to become a little more rational, and we can train ourselves to use our language as an instrument not of self-expression (as our romantic educationists would say) but of rational communication. History itself—I mean the history of power politics, of course, not the non-existent story of the development of mankind—has no end nor meaning, but we can decide to give it both. We can make it our fight for the open society and against its enemies (who, when in a corner, always protest their humanitarian sentiments, in accordance with Pareto's advice) ; and we can interpret it accordingly. Ultimately, we may say the same about the "meaning of life." It is up to us to decide what shall be our purpose in life, to determine our ends.

This dualism of facts and decisions is, I believe, fundamental. Facts as such have no meaning; they can gain it only through our decisions. Historicism is only one of many attempts to get over this dualism; it is born of fear, for it shrinks from realizing that we bear the ultimate responsibility even for the standards we choose. But such an attempt seems to me to represent precisely what is usually described as superstition. For it assumes that we can reap where we have not sown; it tries to persuade us that if we merely fall into step with history everything will and must go right, and that no fundamental decision on our part is required; it tries to shift our responsibility on to history, and thereby on to the play of demoniac powers beyond ourselves; it tries to base our actions upon the hidden intentions of these powers, which can be revealed to us only in mystical inspirations and intuitions; and it thus puts our actions and ourselves on the moral level of a man who, inspired by horoscopes and dreams, chooses his lucky number in a lottery. Like gambling, historicism is born of our despair in the rationality and responsibility of our actions. It is a debased hope and a debased faith, an attempt to replace the hope and the faith that springs from our moral enthusiasm and the contempt for success by a certainty that springs from a pseudo-science; a pseudo-science of the stars, or of "human nature," or of historical destiny.

Historicism, I assert, is not only rationally untenable, it is also in conflict with any religion that teaches the importance of conscience. For such a religion must agree with the rationalist attitude towards history in its emphasis on our supreme responsibility for our actions, and for their repercussions upon the course of history. True, we need hope; to act, to live without hope goes beyond our strength. But we do *not* need more, and we must not be given more. We do not need certainty. Religion, in particular, should not be a substitute for dreams and wish-fulfilment; it should resemble neither the holding of a ticket in a lottery, nor the holding of a policy in an insurance company. The historicist element in religion is an element of idolatry, of superstition.

This emphasis upon the dualism of facts and decisions determines also our attitude towards such ideas as "progress." If we think that history progresses, or that we are bound to progress, then we commit the same mistake as those who believe that history has a meaning that can be discovered in it and need not be given to it. For to progress is to move towards some kind of end, towards an end which exists for us as human beings. "History" cannot do that; only we, the human individuals, can do it; we can do it by defending and strengthening those democratic institutions upon which freedom, and with it progress, depends. And we shall do it much better as we become more fully aware of the fact that progress rests with us, with our watchfulness, with our efforts, with the clarity of our conception of our ends, and with the realism of their choice.

Instead of posing as prophets we must become the makers of our fate. We must learn to do things as well as we can, and to look out for our mistakes. And when we have dropped the idea that the history of power will be our judge, when we have given up worrying whether or not history will justify us, then one day perhaps we may succeed in getting power under control. In this way we may even justify history, in our turn. It badly needs a justification.

ISAIAH BERLIN

Historical Inevitability

We have spoken thus far of the view that we cannot praise or blame because we know, or shall soon know, or at any rate could know, too much for that. By a queer paradox the same position is reached by those who hold what seems at first the diametrical opposite of this position, that we cannot praise or blame, not because we know too much, but because we know too little. Historians imbued with a sense of humility before the scope and difficulties of their task, viewing the magnitude of human claims and the smallness of human knowledge and wisdom, warn us sternly against setting up our parochial values as universally valid and applying what may, at most, hold for a small portion of humanity for a brief span, in some insignificant corner of the universe, to all beings in all places and at all times. Tough-minded realists influenced by Marxism and Christian apologists differ profoundly in outlook, in method, in conclusions, but they are at one in this. The former[1] tell us that the social or economic principles, which, for example, Victorian Englishmen accepted as

---

[1]See, for example, the impressive and influential writings of Mr. E. H. Carr on the history of our time.

From *Historical Inevitability* by Isaiah Berlin (London, 1954), published by Oxford University Press, pp. 43–53.

158

basic and eternal, were but the interests of one particular island community at one particular moment of its social and commercial development, and the truths which they so dogmatically bound upon themselves and upon others, and in the name of which they felt justified in acting as they did, were but their own passing economic or political needs and claims, masquerading as universal truths, and rang progressively more hollow in the ears of other nations with increasingly opposed interests, as they found themselves frequently the losers in a game where the rules had been invented by the stronger side. Then the day began to dawn when they in their turn acquired sufficient power, and turned the tables, and transformed international morality, albeit unconsciously, to suit themselves. Nothing is absolute, moral rules vary directly as the distribution of power: the prevalent morality is always that of the victors; we cannot pretend to hold the scales of justice even between them and their victims, for we ourselves belong to one side or the other; *ex hypothesi* we cannot see the world from more than one vantage point at a time. If we insist on judging others in terms of our transient standards we must not protest too much if they, in their turn, judge us in terms of theirs, which sanctimonious persons among us are too swift to denounce for no better reason than that they are not ours. Some Christian opponents of this position, starting from very different assumptions, see men as feeble creatures groping in darkness, knowing but little of how things come about, or what in history inexorably causes what, and how things might have turned out, but for this or that scarcely perceptible, all but untraceable, fact or situation. Men, they argue, often seek to do what is right according to their lights, but these lights are dim, and such faint illumination as they give reveal very different aspects of life to different observers. The English follow their own traditions; the Germans fight for the development of theirs; the Russians to break with their own and those of other nations; and the result is often bloodshed, widespread suffering, the destruction of what is most highly valued in the various cultures which come into violent conflict. Man proposes, but it is cruel and absurd to lay upon him—poor, fragile creature, born to sorrows—responsibility for many of the disasters that occur. For these are entailed by what, to take a Christian historian of distinction, Professor Herbert Butterfield calls the "human predicament" itself—wherein we seem to ourselves virtuous enough, but being imperfect, and doomed to stay so by Man's original sin, being ignorant, hasty, vainglorious, self-centred, lose our way, do unwitting harm, destroy what we seek to save and strengthen what we seek to destroy. If we understood more, perhaps we could do better, but our intellect is imperfect. For Professor Butterfield, if I understand him correctly, the "human predicament" is a product of the complex interaction of innumerable factors, few among them known, fewer still controllable, the greater number scarcely recognized at all. The least that we can do, therefore, is to acknowledge our condition with due humility; and since we are involved in a common darkness, and few of us stumble in it to much greater purpose than others (at least in the perspective of the whole of human history), we should practise understanding and charity. The least we can do as historians, scrupulous to say no more than we are entitled to say, is to suspend judgment; neither praise nor condemn; for the evidence is always insufficient, and the alleged culprits are like swimmers for ever caught in cross-currents and whirlpools beyond their control.

A not dissimilar philosophy, it seems to me, is to be found in the writings of Tolstoy and other pessimists and quietists, both religious and irreligious. For these, particularly those conservatives of our own day who echo Hume or Burke or Taine, life is a stream moving in a given direction, or perhaps a tideless ocean stirred by occasional breezes. The number of factors which cause it to be as it is, is very great, but we know only a small number of them. To seek to alter things radically in terms of our knowledge is therefore often unrealistic to the point of absurdity; we cannot resist the central currents, for they are stronger than we, we can only tack, trim to the winds and avoid collisions with the great fixed institutions of our world, its physical and biological laws, and the great human establishments with their roots deep in the past—the empires, the churches, the settled beliefs and habits of mankind. For if we resist these our small craft will be sunk, and we shall lose our lives to no purpose. Wisdom lies in avoiding situations where we may capsize, in using the winds that blow as skilfully as we can, so that we may last at any rate our own time, preserve the heritage of the past, and not hurry towards a future, which will come soon enough, and may be darker even than the gloomy present. On this view, more common, perhaps, in our time than in the past, it is the human predicament—the disproportion between our vast designs and our feeble means—that is responsible for most of the suffering and injustice of the world. Without help, without divine grace, or one or other form of divine intervention, we shall not, in any case, succeed. Let us then be tolerant and charitable and understanding, and avoid the folly of accusation and counter-accusation, which will expose us to the laughter or pity of later generations. Let us seek to discern what we can—some dim outline of a pattern—in the shadows of the past, for even so much is surely difficult enough.

In one important sense, of course, such hard-boiled realists and Christian historians are right. Censoriousness, recrimination, moral or emotional blindness to the ways of life and outlooks of others, intellectual or ethical fanaticism, are vices in the writing of history, as in life. No doubt Gibbon and Michelet and Macaulay and Carlyle and Treitschke and Trotsky (to mention only the dead) do try the patience of those who do not accept their opinions, almost beyond endurance. Nevertheless this corrective to dogmatic partiality, like its opposite, the doctrine of inevitable bias, by shifting responsibility on to human weakness and ignorance, and identifying the human predicament itself as the ultimate central factor in human history, in the end leads us by a different road to the very same position as the doctrine that to know all is to forgive all; only for the latter it substitutes the formula that the less we know the fewer reasons we can have for just condemnation; for knowledge can only lead to a clearer realization of how small a part men's wishes and even their unconscious desires play in the life of the universe, and thereby reveals the absurdity of placing any serious responsibility upon the shoulders of individuals, or, for that matter, of classes, or states, or nations.

Two separate strands of thought are involved in the modern plea for a greater effort at understanding and the fashionable warnings against censoriousness, moralizing, and partisan history.

There is, in the first place, the view that men and nations always, or at any rate more often than not, aim at what seems to them desirable; but owing to ignorance, or weakness, or the complexities of the world which mere human insight and skill cannot adequately understand or control, they feel and act in such a manner that the result is too often disastrous both for themselves and for others, caught in the common human predicament. Yet it is not individuals but the human predicament itself—man's imperfection—that is largely to blame for this. There is, in the second place, the further thesis that in attempting to explain historical situations and to analyse them, to unwind their origins and trace their consequences, and, in the course of this, to fix the responsibility for this or that element in the situation, the historian, no matter how detached, clear-headed, scrupulous, dispassionate, however skilled at imagining himself in other men's shoes, is nevertheless faced with a network of facts so minute, connected by links so many and complex, that his ignorance must always far outweigh his knowledge; consequently his judgment, particularly his moral judgment, must always be founded on insufficient data; and if he succeeds in casting even a little light upon some small corner of the vast and intricate pattern of the past, he has done as well as any human being can ever hope to do. The difficulties of disentangling even a minute portion of the truth are so great that he must, if he is an honest and serious practitioner, soon realize how far he is from being in a position to moralize. Consequently to praise and blame, as historians and publicists do so easily and glibly, is presumptuous, foolish, irresponsible, unjust. This *prima facie* very convincing thesis[2] is, however, not one but two: It is one thing to say that man proposes, but the consequences are too often beyond his control or powers of prediction or prevention; that since human motives have so seldom had any decisive influence on the actual course of events, they should not play any great part in the accounts of the historian; and that since the historian's business is to discover and describe what occurred, and how and why, therefore if he allows

[2]Held, unless I have gravely misunderstood his writings, by Professor Herbert Butterfield.

his moral opinions of men's characters and motives—those least effective of all historical factors—to colour his interpretations, he is thereby exaggerating their importance for purely subjective or psychological reasons; for to treat what may be morally significant as *eo ipso* historically influential is to distort the facts. That is a perfectly clear position. Quite distinct from it is the other thesis, namely, that our knowledge is never sufficient to justify us in fixing responsibility, if there is any, where it truly belongs. An omniscient being could do so, but we are not onmiscient, and our attributions are therefore absurdly presumptuous; to realize this and feel an appropriate degree of humility is the beginning of historical wisdom. It may well be that both these theses are true. And it may further be that they both spring from the same kind of pessimistic conviction of human weakness, blindness and ineffectiveness both in thought and in action. Nevertheless, these melancholy views are two, not one: the first is an argument from ineffectiveness, the second from ignorance: and either might be true and the other false. Moreover, neither seems to accord with common belief, nor with the common practice of either ordinary men or of ordinary historians; each seems plausible and unplausible in its own way, and each deserves its own refutation. And I should like to draw attention to an implication common to them: in both these doctrines individual responsibility is made to melt away. We may not applaud nor condemn individuals or groups either because they cannot help themselves (and all knowledge is a growing understanding of precisely this), or conversely because we know too little to know either this or its opposite. But then neither may we bring charges of moralism or bias against those historians who are prone to praise and blame, because we are all in the same boat together, and no one standard can be called objectively superior to any other. For what, on this view, could "objective" mean? and by what standard do we measure its degrees? It is plain that there can exist no "super-standard" for the comparison of entire scales of value, which itself derives from no specific set of beliefs, no one specific culture. All such tests must be internal, like the laws of a state that apply only to its own citizens. The case against the notion of historical objectivity is like the case against international law or international morality: that it does not exist. And more than this: that the very notion has no meaning, because ultimate standards are what we measure things by, and cannot by definition themselves be measured in terms of anything else.

This is indeed to be hoist by one's own petard. Because all standards are relative, to condemn bias or moralism in history or to defend them, turn out themselves to be attitudes which, in the absence of a super-standard, cannot be rationally defended or condemned. All attitudes turn out to be morally neutral; but even this cannot be said, for the contradictory of this proposition cannot be refuted. Hence nothing on this topic can be said at all. This is surely a *reductio ad absurdum* of the entire position. A fallacy must be lurking somewhere in the argument of the anti-moralistic school.[3]

[3]The paradox arising out of general scepticism about historical objectivity may perhaps be put in another fashion. One of the principal reasons for complaining about the moralistic attitude of this or that historian is that his scale of values is thought to distort his judgments, to cause him to pervert the truth. But if we start from the assumption that historians, like other human beings, are wholly conditioned to think as they do by specific material (or immaterial factors, however incalculable or impalpable, then their so-called bias is, like everything else about their thought, the inevitable consequence of their material or "ontological" predicament, and so, equally, are our objections to it—our own ideals of impartiality, our own standards of objective truth in terms of which we condemn, say, nationalistic or Marxist historians, or other forms of animus or *parti pris*. For what is sauce for the subjective goose must be sauce for the objective gander; if we look at the matter from the vantage point of a Marxist or a Fascist, our "objective" attitude is an equal offence against their standards, which is, in their own eyes, no less self-evident, absolute, valid, &c. In this relativistic view the very notion of an absolute standard, presupposing as it does the rejection of all specific vantage points as such, must, of course, be an absurdity. All complaints about partiality and bias, about moral (or political) propaganda seem, on this view, beside the point. Whatever dies not agree with our views we call misleading, but if this fault is to be called subjectivism, so must the condemnation of it; it ought to follow that no point of view is superior to any other, save in so far as it proceeds from wider knowledge (given that there is a commonly agreed standard for measuring such width). We are what we are, and when and where we are; and when we are historians, we select and emphasize, interpret and evaluate, reconstruct and present facts, as we do, each in his own way. On this view all that we do when we reject this or that historian as a conscious or unconscious propagandist, is solely to indicate our own moral or intellectual or historical distance from him; nothing more: we are merely underlining our personal

Let us consider the normal thoughts of ordinary men on this topic. In normal circumstances we do not feel that we are saying something hazardous or questionable if we praise or condemn Cromwell for what he did for the English, or if we describe Pasteur as a benefactor of mankind or Hitler as an evil-doer. Nor do we feel that we are saying something strange if we maintain that, let us say, the late Mr. Belloc or Lord Macaulay do not seem to apply the same standards of objective truth, or apply them as impartially, as did, let us say, Ranke, or Bishop Creighton, or M. Elie Halévy. In saying this, what are we asserting? Are we merely expressing our private approval or disapproval of Cromwell's acts or Pasteur's purposes or our distaste for Hitler's character or activities? Are we merely saying that we agree with Ranke's conclusions or M. Halévy's general tone, that they are more to our taste, please us better (because of our own outlook and temperament) than the tone and conclusions of Macaulay or Mr. Belloc? Yet if there is an unmistakable tinge of reproach in our assessment of, say, Cromwell's policies or of Mr. Belloc's account of those policies, is that no more than an indication that we are not favourably disposed towards one or other of them, that our moral or intellectual ideals differ from what we take to be theirs, with no indication that we think that they could, and moreover should, have acted differently? And if we do imply that their behaviour might, or should, have been different, is that merely a symptom of our psychological inability to realize that they could not (for no one can) have acted differently, or of an ignorance too deep to entitle us to tell how they could, let alone should, have acted? With the further implication that it would be more civilized not to say such things, but to remember that we are all equally, or almost equally, deluded, and remember, too, that moral responsibility is a fiction, that with the increase of knowledge and a more scrupulous and appropriate use of language, such quasi-ethical expressions, and the false notions of human

---

position. And this seems to be a fatal internal contradiction within the system of those who believe in the historical conditioning of historians and yet protest against moralizing by them, whether ironically like Mr. Carr, or sorrowfully like Professor Butterfield.

freedom on which they rest, will, it is to be hoped, finally disappear from the vocabulary of civilized human beings? For this seems to me to follow directly from the doctrines outlined above. Determinism, whether benevolent or malevolent, no less than the view that our moral judgments are rendered absurd either because we know too much or because we know too little, all seem to point to this: it is a view that in its various forms has been held by many civilized and sensitive persons. Nevertheless it rests on beliefs about the world and about human beings which are too difficult to accept; which are unplausible because they render illegitimate certain basic distinctions which we all draw— distinctions which are inevitably reflected in our everyday use of words. If such beliefs were true, too much that we accept without question would turn out to be sensationally false. Yet these paradoxes are urged upon us although there is no evidence to force us to embrace them.

It is part of the same tendency to maintain that even if total freedom from moralizing is not to be looked for in this world (for all human beings inevitably live and think by their own varying moral or aesthetic or religious standards) yet, as historians, an effort must be made to repress such tendencies. As historians it is our duty only to describe and explain, not to pronounce verdicts. The historian is, we are told, not a judge but a detective; he provides the evidence, and the reader, who has none of the professional responsibilities of the expert, can form what moral conclusions he likes. As a general warning against moralistic history this is, particularly in times of acute partisan emotion, timely enough. But it must not be interpreted literally. For it depends upon a false analogy with some among the more exact of the natural sciences. In these last objectivity has a specific meaning. It means that methods and criteria of a less or more precisely defined kind are being used with scrupulous care; and that evidence, arguments, conclusions are formulated in the special terminology invented or employed for the specific purpose of each science, and that there is no intrusion (or almost none) of irrelevant considerations, or concepts or categories, i.e. those specifically excluded by the canons of the science in question. I am not sure whether history can usefully be called a science at all, but certainly it is not a science in this sense. For it employs few, if any, concepts or categories peculiar to itself, but broadly speaking, only those of common sense, or of ordinary speech. The central concepts of history—the ways in which events or situations are "explained," are shown to be connected or unconnected with one another—the use of such crucial terms as "because" and "therefore," "inevitable" and "possible" and "probable," "surprising" and "unexpected," "influential" and "trival," "central" and "accidental," and so forth, is much the same as that which it has in ordinary, non-technical thought and speech. As history becomes specialized, e.g. in such disciplines as the history of science or of commerce or of art, technical terms do begin to make their appearance, and to that degree something approaching, but still somewhat remotely, the natural sciences, begins to occur, and the elimination of a good many of the normal moral and psychological concepts of daily speech becomes possible and, according to some, desirable and perhaps even indispensable. But in the realm of general history, social, political, and cultural—what goes by the name of history without specific qualification—this is not so. There we explain and elucidate as we explain and elucidate in ordinary life. We account for the French Revolution or the character of Napoleon or the behaviour of Talleyrand as we would account for the behaviour of our own contemporaries and events in our own lives, public and private, with the same rich, scarcely analyzable mixture of physiological and psychological, economic and biographical, aesthetic and ethical, causal and purposive concepts, which provide what we regard as normal and sufficient answers to our normal questions about how and why things or persons act as they do. All attempts to construct special sets of concepts and special techniques for history (e.g. by Marxists) have broken down because they proved sterile, for they either misdescribed—overschematized—our experience, or they were felt not to provide answers to our questions. We can accuse historians of bias, or inaccuracy, or stupidity, or dishonesty, as we can accuse one another of these vices in our ordinary daily intercourse; and usually with the same degree of justice and reason. But just as our ordinary speech would become fantastically distorted by a conscious effort to eliminate from it some basic

ingredient—say, everything remotely liable to convey value judgments, our normal, scarcely noticed, moral or psychological attitudes—and just as this is not regarded as indispensable for the
preservation of what we should look upon as a normal modicum
of objectivity, impartiality, and accuracy, so, for the same reason,
no such radical remedy is needed for the preservation of a reasonable modicum of these qualities in the writing of history.
There is a sense in which a physicist can, to a large degree, speak
with different voices, as a physicist, and as a human being;
although even there the line between the two vocabularies is
anything but clear or absolute. It is possible that this may in some
measure be true of economists or psychologists; it grows progressively less true as we leave mathematical methods behind us, for
example, in palaeography, or the history of science or that of the
woollen trade; and it comes perilously near an absurdity when
demanded of social or political historians, however skilled in the
appropriate techniques, however professional, however rigorous.
History is not identical with imaginative literature, but it is certainly no more free from what, in a natural science, would be
rightly condemned as unwarrantably subjective or personal. Except on the assumption that history must deal with human beings
purely as material objects in space—must, in short, be behaviourist—its method can scarcely be assimilated to the standards of an
exact natural science.[4] The invocation to historians to suppress
even the minimal degree of moral or psychological evaluation

[4]That history is in this sense different from physical description, is a truth
discovered long ago by Vico, and most imaginatively and vividly presented by
Herder and his followers, and, despite the exaggerations and extravagances to
which it led some nineteenth-century philosophers of history, still remains the
greatest contribution of the Romantic movement to our knowledge. What was then
shown, albeit often in a very misleading and confused fashion, was that to reduce
history to a natural science was deliberately to leave out of account what we know
to be true, to suppress great portions of our most familiar introspective knowledge
on the altar of a false analogy with the sciences and their mathematical and
scientific disciplines. This exhortation to the students of humanity to practise
austerities, and commit deliberate acts of self-laceration, that like Origen, they
might escape all temptation to sin (involved in any lapse from "neutral" protocols
of the data of observation) is to render the writing of history at once pathetic and
ridiculous.

which is necessarily involved in viewing human beings as creatures with purposes and motives (and not merely as causal factors in the procession of events), seems to me to rest upon a confusion of the aims and methods of the humane studies with those of natural science. It is one of the greatest and most destructive fallacies of the last hundred years.

On Fortune and Misfortune in History

The conception of a happiness which consists in the permanence of certain conditions is of its very nature false. The moment we set aside a primitive state, or state of nature, in which every day is like every other day, and every century like every other century, until, by some rupture, historical life begins, we must admit that permanence means paralysis and death. Only in movement with all its pain, is life. And above all, the idea of happiness as a positive feeling is false in itself. Happiness is mere absence of pain, at best associated with a faint sense of growth.

There have been, of course, arrested peoples who present the same general picture for centuries and hence give the impression of tolerable contentment with their fate. As a rule, however, that is the product of despotism, which inevitably appears when a form of State and society has been achieved (presumably at great cost) and has to be defended against the rise of opposing forces, and with all available measures, even the most extreme. The first generation must, as a rule, have been very unhappy, but suceeding ones grow up in that order of ideas, and ultimately they pronounce sacred everything that they cannot and do not wish to change, praising it perhaps as supreme happiness. When Spain was on the point of material extinction, she was still capable of deep feeling as soon as the splendor of the Castilian name came into question. The oppression of the government and the Inquisition seems to have been powerless to humiliate her soul. Her greatest artists and poets belong to that age.

These stationary peoples and national epochs may exist in order to preserve definite spiritual, intellectual and material values from earlier times and to pass them on uncontaminated as a leaven to the future. And their calm is not absolute and deathly; it is rather of the nature of a refreshing sleep.

There are other ages, peoples, men, on the other hand, which at times spend their strength, indeed their whole strength, in rapid movement. Their importance resides in the destruction of the old and the clearing of the way for the new. But they were not made for any lasting happiness, or indeed for any passing joy, save for the short-lived rejoicing of victory. For their power of regeneration is born of perpetual discontent, which finds any halt tedious and demands to advance.

Now this striving, however important its consequences, however great its political consequences may be, actually appears in time in the garb of the most unfathomable human egoism, which must of necessity subdue others to its will and find its satisfaction in their obedience, yet which is insatiable in its thirst for obedience and admiration and claims the right to use force in all great issues.

Now evil on earth is assuredly a part of the great economy of world history. It is force, the right of the stronger over the weaker, prefigured in that struggle for life which fills all nature, the animal and the vegetable worlds, and is carried on in the early stages of humanity by murder and robbery, by the eviction, extermination or enslavement of weaker races, or of weaker peoples within the same race, of weaker States, of weaker social classes within the same State and people.

Yet the stronger, as such, is far from being the better. Even in the vegetable kingdom, we can see baser and bolder species making headway here and there. In history, however, the defeat of the noble simply because it is in the minority is a grave danger, especially in times ruled by a very general culture which arrogates to itself the rights of the majority. The forces which have succumbed were perhaps nobler and better, but the victorious, though their only motive was ambition, inaugurate a future of which they themselves have no inkling. Only in the exemption of States from the general moral law, which continues to be binding on the individual, can something like a premonition of it be divined.

The greatest example is offered by the Roman Empire, inaugurated by the most frightful methods soon after the end of the struggle between the patricians and plebeians in the guise of the Samnite War, and completed by the subjection of East and West in rivers of blood.

Here, on the grand scale, we can discern a historical purpose which is, to us at any rate, plainly apparent, namely the creation of a common world culture, which also made possible the spread of a world religion, both capable of being transmitted to the Teutonic barbarians of the Völkerwanderung as the future bond of a new Europe.

Yet from the fact that good came of evil, and relative happiness of misery, we cannot in any way deduce that evil and misery were not, at the outset, what they were. Every successful act of violence is evil, and at the very least a dangerous example. But when that act was the foundation of power, it was followed by the indefatigable efforts of men to turn mere power into law and order. With their healthy strength, they set to work to cure the State of violence.

And, at times, evil reigns long as evil on earth, and not only among Fatimids and Assassins. According to Christian doctrine, the prince of this world is Satan. There is nothing more unchristian than to promise virtue a lasting reign, a material divine reward here below, as the early Church writers did to the Christian Emperors. Yet evil, as ruler, is of supreme importance; it is the one condition of selfless good. It would be a horrible sight if, as a result of the consistent reward of good and punishment of evil on this earth, all men were to behave well with an ulterior motive, for they would continue to be evil men and to nourish evil in their hearts. The time might come when men would pray Heaven for a little impunity for evildoers, simply in order that they might show their real nature once more. There is enough hypocrisy in the world as it is.

Let us now try to see whether the consolation we have divined will stand the test of a few of the most justified indictments of history.

Firstly, by no means every destruction entails regeneration. Just as the destruction of a finer vegetation may turn a land into an arid waste forever, a people which has been too brutally handled will never recover. There are (or at any rate there seem to be) absolutely destructive forces under whose hoofs no grass grows. The essential strength of Asia seems to have been permanently and for ever broken by the two periods of Mongol rule. Timur in particular was horribly devastating with his pyramids of skulls and walls of lime, stone and living men. Confronted with the picture of the destroyer, as he parades his own and his people's self-seeking through the world, it is good to realize the irresistible might with which evil may at times spread over the world. In such countries, men will never again believe in right and human kindness. Yet he may have saved Europe from the Osmanlis. Imagine history without him, and Bajazet and the Hussites hurling themselves simultaneously on Germany and Italy. The later Osmanlis, people and sultans, whatever terror they may have meant for Europe, never again approach the climax of power represented by Bajazet I before the battle of Angora.

Even ancient times present a picture of horror when we imagine the sum of despair and misery which went to establish the old world Empires, for instance. Our deepest compassion, perhaps, would go out to those individual peoples who must have succumbed to the Kings of Persia, or even to the Kings of Assyria and Media, in their desperate struggle for independence. All the lonely royal fortresses of individual peoples (Hyrcanians, Bactrians, Sogdanians, Gedrosians) which Alexander encountered marked the scenes of ghastly last struggles, of which all knowledge has been lost. Did they fight in vain?

We feel quite differently about the peoples whose last struggle and end are known to us; that of the Lydian cities against Harpagus, Carthage, Numantia, Jerusalem against Titus. They seem to us to have taken their place in the ranks of those who have been the teachers and examples of mankind in the one great cause—that all must be staked on the cause of the whole and that individual life is not the supreme value. And thus, of their despair, a happiness, harsh but sublime, is born for all the world.

And if Persian tablets should be discovered bringing us greater knowledge of the end of those peoples in the Eastern provinces, were they only conceived in the bombastic Ormuzd style of the mindless victor, they would go to swell the number of those great memories.

We may here leave out of account the consolation we derive from the thought that without such temporary destroyers as Assyria and Persia, Alexander could not have borne the elements of Greek culture so far into Asia. Beyond Mesopotamia it had little influence. We must always be on our guard against taking our historical perspectives for the decrees of history.

One thing, however, must be said of all great destructions: since we cannot fathom the economy of world history, we never know what would have happened if some event, however terrible, had not occurred. Instead of one wave of history which we know, another, which we do not know, would have risen; instead of one evil oppressor, perhaps one still more evil.

Yet no man of power should imagine that he can put forward for his exculpation the plea: "If we do not do it, others will." For then every crime would be justified. (Such men in any case feel no need of exculpation, but say: "What *we* do turns out well because *we* do it.")

It may be, too, that if those who succumbed had lived longer, they would no longer have seemed worthy of our compassion. A people, for instance, that succumbed early in the glorious struggle might later not have been very happy, not very civilized, early corrupted by its own iniquity and deadly to its neighbors. But, having perished in the flower of its strength, we feel toward it as we feel toward exceptional men who have died young; we imagine that, had they lived, they could not but have progressed in good fortune and greatness, while perhaps their meridian already lay behind them.

Consolation comes from another direction in the mysterious law of compensation, which becomes apparent in one point at least, namely in the increase of populations after great plagues and wars. There seems to be a total life of humanity which makes losses good.

Thus it is not certain, yet it appears to us probable, that the retreat of culture from the eastern half of the Mediterranean in the fifteenth century was made good, spiritually and materially, by the expansion overseas of the peoples of Western Europe. The accent of the world shifted.

Thus as, in the one case, another manner of death would have come instead of the one we know, in this case the vital power of the world replaces a vanished life by a new one.

The compensation, however, must not be taken as a substitute for suffering, to which its originator might point, but only as a continuance of the life of wounded humanity with its center of gravity shifted. Not must we hold it out to the sufferers and their dependents. The Völkerwanderung was a great rejuvenation for the moribund Roman Empire, but if we had asked the Byzantine, living under the Comneni in the twelfth century in the Eastern remnant of it, he would have spoken with all the pride in the world of the continued life of Rome on the Bosphorus, and with an equal contempt of the "renewed and refreshed" Occident. Even the Greco-Slav of our day under the Turks does not consider himself inferior to, and probably not more unhappy than, the man of the West. Indeed, if the people were consulted, they could not pay for the greatest regeneration in the world, if the price were their own end and the influx of savage hordes.

The theory of compensation is, after all, generally the theory of desirability in disguise, and it is and remains advisable to be exceedingly chary in the use of such consolation as is to be gained from it, since we cannot finally assess these losses and gains. Bloom and decay are certainly the common lot, but every really personal life that is cut off by violence, and (in our opinion) prematurely, must be regarded as absolutely irreplaceable, indeed as irreplaceable even by one of equal excellence.

Another variant of compensation is the postponement of an event which seemed imminent. From time to time a great event, ardently desired, does not take place because some future time will fulfil it in greater perfection. In the Thirty Years' War, Germany was twice on the point of union, in 1629 by Wallenstein, in 1631 by Gustavus Adolphus. In both cases a terrible, unbridgeable breach would have remained in the nation. The birth of the nation was postponed for 240 years, and came at a moment when that breach had ceased to be a menace. In the realm of art we may say that Pope Nicholas V's new St. Peter's would have been immeasurably inferior to the St. Peter's of Bramante and Michelangelo.

Another variant is the substitution of one branch of culture for another. In the first half of the eighteenth century, when poetry was almost completely negligible and painting half dead, music reached its sublimest heights. Yet here too there are imponderabilia which we must not play off against each other too glibly. The one thing certain is that *one* time, *one* people cannot possess everything at the same time, and that a great many talents, of themselves indeterminate, are attracted by the art that has already reached its zenith.

The most justified indictments which we seem to have the right to bring against fate are those which concern the destruction of great works of art and literature. We might possibly be ready to forgo the learning of the ancient world, the libraries of Alexandria and Pergamum; we have enough to do to cope with the learning of modern times, but we mourn for the supreme poets whose works have been lost, and the historians too represent an irreparable loss because the continuity of intellectual tradition has become fragmentary over long and important periods. But that continuity is a prime concern of man's earthly life, and a metaphysical proof of the significance of its duration, for whether a spiritual continuity existed without our knowledge, in an organ unknown to us, we cannot tell, and in any case cannot imagine it, hence we most urgently desire that the awareness of that continuity should remain living in our minds.

Yet our unfulfilled longing for the lost is worth something too. We owe to it, and to it alone, the fact that so many fragments have been rescued and pieced together by incessant study. Indeed, the worship of relics of art and the indefatigable combination of the relics of history form part of the religion of our day.

Our capacity for worship is as important as the object we worship.

It may be, too, that those great works of art had to perish in order that later art might create in freedom. For instance, if, in the fifteenth century, vast numbers of well-preserved Greek sculptures and paintings had been discovered, Leonardo, Raphael, Titian and Correggio would not have done their work, while they could, in their own way, sustain the comparison with what had been inherited from Rome. And if, after the middle of the eighteenth century, in the enthusiastic revival of philological and antiquarian studies, the lost Greek lyric poets had suddenly been rediscovered, they might well have blighted the full flowering of German poetry. It is true that, after some decades, the mass of rediscovered ancient poetry would have become assimilated with it, but the decisive moment of bloom, which never returns in its full prime, would have been irretrievably past. But enough had survived in the fifteenth century for art, and in the eighteenth for poetry, to be stimulated and not stifled.

Having reached this point, we must stop. Imperceptibly we have passed from the question of good and evil fortune to that of the survival of the human spirit, which in the end presents itself to us as the life of *one* human being. That life, as it becomes self-conscious *in* and *through* history, cannot fail in time so to fascinate the gaze of the thinking man, and the study of it so to engage his power, that the ideas of fortune and misfortune inevitably fade. "Ripeness is all." Instead of happiness, the able mind will, *nolens volens,* take knowledge as its goal. Nor does that happen from indifference to a wretchedness that may befall us too—whereby we are guarded against all pretense of cool detachment—but because we realize the blindness of our desires, since the desires of peoples and of individuals neutralize each other.

If we could shake off our individuality and contemplate the history of the immediate future with exactly the same detachment and agitation as we bring to a spectacle of nature—for instance, a storm at sea seen from land—we should perhaps experience in full consciousness one of the greatest chapters in the history of the human mind.

At a time when the illusory peace of thirty years in which we grew up has long since utterly vanished, and a series of fresh wars seems to be imminent;

when the established political forms of the greatest civilized peoples are tottering or changing;

when, with the spread of education and communications, the realization and impatience of suffering is visibly and rapidly growing;

when social institutions are being shaken to their foundations by world movements, not to speak of all the accumulated crises which have not yet found their issues;

it would be a marvelous spectacle—though not for contemporary earthly beings—to follow with enlightened perception the spirit of man as it builds its new dwelling, soaring above, yet closely bound up with all these manifestations. Any man with such a vision in mind would completely forget about fortune and misfortune, and would spend his life in the quest of that knowledge.

SELECTED READINGS

Aron, R., *Introduction to the Philosophy of History,* translated by G. Irwin, Boston, 1961.

Barraclough, G., *History in a Changing World,* Oxford, Eng., 1955.

Becker, C. L., *Everyman His Own Historian,* New York, 1935.

————, *Progress and Power,* Stanford, Calif., 1936.

Berdyaev, N., *The Meaning of History,* London, 1936.

Bloch, M., *The Historian's Craft,* translated by P. Putnam, New York, 1953.

Bultmann, R., *History and Eschatology,* Edinburgh, 1957.

Butterfield, H., *Christianity and History,* New York, 1950.

————, *The Whig Interpretation of History,* New York, 1951.

Cassirer, E., *The Problem of Knowledge: Philosophy, Science, and History Since Hegel,* New Haven, Conn., 1950.

Cohen, M. R., *The Meaning of History,* La Salle, Ill., 1947.

Dawson, C., *The Dynamics of World History,* New York, 1962.

Dilthey, W., *Pattern and Meaning in History,* H. P. Rickman, ed., New York, 1962.

Dray, W., *Laws and Explanation in History,* London, 1957.

————(ed.), *Philosophical Analysis and History,* New York, 1966.

Elton, G. R., *The Practise of History,* New York, 1967.

Gardiner, P., *The Nature of Historical Explanation,* New York, 1955.

————, *Theories of History,* New York, 1959.

Geyl, P., *The Use and Abuse of History,* New Haven, Conn., 1955.

Gooch, G. P., *History and Historians in the Nineteenth Century,* London, 1913.

Gottschalk, L., *Understanding History,* New York, 1950.

Hempel, G. G., "The Function of General Laws in History," *Journal of Philosophy,* XXXIX, 1942, pp. 35–48.

Hexter, J. H., *Reappraisals in History,* Evanston, Ill., 1961.

Jaspers, K., *The Origin and Goal of History,* New Haven, Conn., 1953.

Klibansky, R., and Paton, H. J., eds., *Philosophy and History,* London, 1936.

Lamprecht, S., *Nature and History,* New York, 1950.

Langlois, C. V., and Seignobos, C., *Introdiction to the Study of History,* tr. G. G. Berry, London, 1912.

Löwith, K., *Meaning in History,* Chicago, 1949.

Mandlebaum, M., *The Problem of Historical Knowledge: An Answer to Relativism,* New York, 1938.

Maritain, J., *On the Philosophy of History,* New York, 1957.

Mazlish, B., *The Riddle of History: The Great Speculators from Vico to Freud,* New York, 1966.

Meyerhoff, H., ed., *The Philosophy of History in Our Time,* New York, 1959.

Muller, H. J., *The Uses of the Past,* New York, 1954.

Nagel, E., *The Structure of Science,* New York, 1961.

Namier, Sir L., *Avenues of History,* London, 1952.

Nietzsche, F., *The Use and Abuse of History,* New York, 1949.

Northrop, F. S. C., *The Logic of the Science and the Humanities,* New York, 1947.

Oman, C., *On the Writing of History,* New York, 1939.

Plekhanov, G. B., *The Materialist Conception of History,* New York, 1940.

Randall, J. H., Jr., *Nature and Historical Experience,* New York, 1958.

Renier, G. J., *History: Its Purpose and Method,* Boston, 1950.

Rowse, A. L., *The Use of History,* London, 1946.

Smith, P., *The Historian and History,* New York, 1960.

"The Social Sciences in Historical Study: A Report of the Committee on Historiography," *SSRC Bulletin* 64, 1954.

Strout, C., *The Pragmatic Revolt in American History,* New Haven, Conn. 1958.

Teggart, F. J., *Theory and Processes of History,* Berkeley, Calif., 1941.

"Theory and Practise in Historical Study: A Report of the Committee on Historiography," *SSRC Bulletin* 54, 1946.

Tholfsen, T. R., *Historical Thinking,* New York, 1967.

Tillich, P., *The Interpretation of History,* New York, 1936.

Vico, G., *The New Science,* translated by T. G. Bergin and M. H. Fisch, Ithaca, N. Y. 1948.

Walsh, W. H., *An Introduction to the Philosophy of History,* London, 1951.

White, M. G., *Foundations of Historical Knowledge,* New York, 1965.